A SWEDISH ADVENTURE IN AMERICA

DAYBOOK JOURNALS OF ALBREKT LUNDQUIST

1910-1924

A SWEDISH ADVENTURE IN AMERICA

To Albrekt Lundquist, my parents, Jane and Arne Lundquist, all of our family, and to all other Immigrants who have struggled to find the "streets of gold" in America, and to John Bartell for encouraging me to publish these memoirs!

Copyright July 2017, Linda-Lundquist Molitor

All rights reserved, including the right to reproduce this book or portions thereof in any form whatsoever. For information contact Linda-Lundquist Molitor, P.O. Box 5775, Elgin, Il 60121

Cover design: Eric Molitor
Translation: Jane and Arne Lundquist
Publisher: Linda-Lundquist Molitor

Edition 1

TABLE OF CONTENTS

Introduction by Linda Lundquist-Molitor   4

Map of California-Cities visited by Albrekt   7

Book 1, Chapter 1 Journey to America   8

Foreword by Albrekt Lundquist   27

Book 1, Chapter 2 Life in America   28

Book 2, Miss Lind's Place   60

Book 3, Kingsburg   92

Book 4, Back to Kingsburg   116

Book 5, Ft. Ross   143

Book 6, Return to Sweden   223

Book 7, Back to America   257

Epilogue by Arne H. Lundquist   272

Photos of family I and II   275

INTRODUCTION

Vill man vara fin får man lida pin. (Swedish proverb)

Meaning: Nothing can be achieved without suffering hardship and adversity.

"JOURNEY TO AMERICA" is the story, written in 7 journals, by my paternal grandfather about his search for success and fortune in America just prior to World War I. It is a story much like the struggles that immigrants and young people are going through today, looking for jobs and a way to make a decent living.

Politics and war have not changed much from then to now either. I agree with his perception of why we have wars—not for the greater good, but for the good of the few!

When I read Grampa's thoughts I am struck by the idea that each generation has had its struggles--and it is the lesson in perseverance and sacrifice that I want to share in this book because that is timeless. I think that my kids and my extended family will be very interested and uplifted by his struggles and how he never quit dreaming in spite of them, and always with his good humor.

I have chosen to not correct the grammar because this is how I remember Grampa speaking---translation is never word for word and grammatically the same as English. He makes a disclaimer of his education in his foreword, which you can read for yourself entitled "My Destiny and Adventures". I think a lot of his words and descriptions are quite eloquent and poetic for a young man of 21 years without a formal education.

I needed to change the *title* of the book due to copy right issues. The cover will be "A SWEDISH ADVENTURE IN AMERICA", but Albrekt titled his journals "JOURNEY TO AMERICA".

I have placed pictures that he took in the early 1900's in the same place as he put them in his journals, even if they were not good pictures. I named the ones I could, but I could not title them all.

I believe that Grampa represents the ideas and values of most Europeans (and others) immigrating to the USA at the beginning of that century. He and all of the other immigrants of those times have contributed to the backbone and fabric of what makes America the "streets of gold" and is the dream others in the rest of the world want to share. ***No one ever said it was easy.***

My mother and father, Jane and Arne Lundquist, translated all of the day books, I have only typed them and formatted them for publishing.

Linda Lundquist-Molitor

MAP OF CALIFORNIA

Cities and Towns Visited by Albrekt

- Weed
- McCloud
- Dunsmuir
- Shasta
- Redding
- Cottonwood
- Oroville
- Sacramento
- Oakland
- Stockton
- Tollhouse
- SAN FRANCISCO
- Merced
- Fresno
- Don Palos
- Sanger
- San Joaquin
- Parlier
- KINGSBURG
- Visalia
- Porter
- LOS ANGELES

BOOK 1

CHAPTER 1

JOURNEY TO AMERICA

March 13, 1910

Ernst Lonkvist (a Swedish American) and myself, left Malmback at 9:00 o'clock tonight. There were a lot of people there. I got a flower bouquet from Dolly Gustafson (the master painter's wife). That was the only one I got, then it was time to leave. We came to Nassjo at 9:30. A lady that rented rooms by the town square met me. We will leave at 7:00 in the morning for Malmo. It is now 10:00 o'clock, so I am going to bed.

March 14, 1910

I got up at 6:00 a.m. and had coffee. The coffee and the room cost $1.25 and the ticket to Malmo cost $6.20. I am writing this while the train is stopped in Savsjo. We left Nassjo at 7:00 o'clock. We have just passed Gavestorps station. We are about 20 immigrants.

I am now in Malmo and have gotten a room at the Skandic Hotel. The cost is $1.50 a day and the coffee is 25 ore. I like Malmo. We got here about 12:50 p.m. Out of all of us that are going to America, I was the only one who had his agent in

Copenhagen. The others were met at the train station, so I had to shift for myself. I left my knapsack in the waiting room and went to find a room. So far, the journey has gone well, as a matter of fact, quite pleasant. The Watch Master is coming from the station with my knapsack. He took it home with him overnight, without charge. I was treated so nice that I was surprised. I have never been treated so nice in Jonkoping.

It is now 7:00 p.m. I went out to look at the town, and now I am tired. I had supper here that cost 1 Crown. That was high for a cutlet, a little potato and milk.

March 15, 1910

We left Malmo at 9:00 o'clock and arrived in Copenhagen at 10:50 and had the company of three Ostergarters. One of them had been in America. They have a pretty little girl with them. She looked to be about 9 or 10 and I just found out that she is only 8. When we got to Copenhagen, the representative for Cunard Lines was there to greet us. He took us through Customs, where we had our luggage marked and tagged. We were shown our room at the Svea Hotel. It was a small room that five people had to share. Supper was served at 5:00 p.m. After that we went out to look at the town. It is both big and beautiful. The King's new street is a nice street. There are shops in every building with full glass fronts. There are buses, cabs and all sorts of transportation.

We were in a bank today. That was the finest room I have ever seen so far. The walls and floors were all marble. Four cornered marble pillars, one meter on each side, rose up to the ceiling. There were about 50 employees in the bank. We were there to get our contract with the agent. Later, we went out in the town, to a biograph theatre and then we went back to the hotel and went to bed.

We got up on the 16th at 6:00 o'clock a.m. and got our baggage in order. We then rode through the whole town on a street car. We wrote down addresses of acquaintances back home, so that the agent could write to them and tell them when we got to New York. We left Copenhagen at 8:30 in the morning and came to the Big Baltic by 10:20. We met five trains on the way. We were on the other side of the big Baltic by 11:50. We were served coffee and sandwiches on the Big Baltic. Later, we traveled through Fyn. There the roads were good and the landscape was pretty with windmills all over. We reached the Little Baltic at 1:15 and crossed over in 15 minutes. We were then packed in small wagons and transported through Jylland. We left there at 2:50 and arrived at Esbjerg at 5:45 where we were examined one by one by a doctor that checked our eyes, checked our contract and stamped our contracts. We then went on board the freighter "Primula" and then we left Esbjerg at 6:30.

March 19th, 1910

The 16th of March, we left Esbjerg and arrived in Harvich at 1:00 o'clock in the morning. The transport over the North Sea was dangerous because there was a terrible storm. Everyone was seasick more or less. I was not too sick, but some were so bad they couldn't talk, or eat, much less vomit. The food we got was poor, a big wooden box full of sandwiches with a little German sausage on them. I ate one sandwich and tasted it the whole trip. As long as I was able to be on deck, I did not have to vomit, but as soon as I had to go below deck into that devilish smell, I did. When it stormed the worst, I was on deck and had to hold on tight so as not to be washed overboard. The water on deck was up to 45 inches high, so I got wet, as tall as I am. I was chased below many times until an old seaman showed me a place on the after deck where I could sit. We left Havich at 1:50 and were in Liverpool at 11:00 o'clock on the 18th. We lived on more sandwiches we got in Havich the rest of the way.

When we got to Liverpool, an agent from Cunard Lines met us with a carriage drawn by two horses. Each carriage held about 20 people with the baggage piled on the roof. When we got to the Cunard Hotel, food was waiting, but no one had much of an appetite. We were then shown our rooms in the hotel. The rooms were nice. We slept two to a bed.

We will leave Liverpool at 5:00 o'clock in the afternoon. Again, we had to show our papers and be accounted for. I am writing this while the boat is in the harbor. I have not been able to write before and I don't know when I'll have a chance again.

It is full of people here. Some have had to go on other boats because there is not enough room for them here. They all want to travel on this boat. There are many that had to go back because their papers were not right. They are very strict now.

March 20, 1910

We have just left the coast of Ireland. Mail and other things were put on the boat there. It is so nice on this boat that one could think he was in a fine hotel. The boat has not started to rock yet. We get served three times a day at beautifully set tables, including flowers. The chairs are on swivels, so when you are finished eating, you just swing around and go on your way.

There are people here from almost the whole of Europe. There are 1900 immigrants and some passengers. Some play cards, some dance, read, smoke, sing and talk. There is a piano down in the dining room that someone is always playing. We are going along Ireland's coast now, so the boat is not rocking, but it surely will once we are out on the Atlantic. Two boys and myself from Smaland have a cabin for four people. It is a fine cabin, among the best on the boat.

March 22, 1910

I was so sick yesterday that I could not write. I am not so well today either, but I will try. It has not stormed much yesterday or today, but I got sick anyway. It is as if your body is broken, and you can hardly eat. The food service is very nice. First you get coffee, then eggs and fish and such. I am already tired of this journey, if only it would end. There is no rest in bed. It is like laying on a log. The pillow is so flat that it is hardly more than a folded blanket. I am sitting in the cabin bed writing with my knapsack as a table. The boat is rocking so bad that I can hardly write. The way it is now, I wish I could have stayed in Sweden. There are some nasty looking people on board, so that you want to vomit just by looking at them. I have never seen so many different kinds of boots and shoes as there are on this boat. There must be twenty-five different kinds. The smell of footwear, along with apples and oranges is so smelly you would not believe it until you have smelled the stench yourself.

We are now vaccinated. We all went up on deck and were so tightly packed together that a young boy fainted from the sultry smell. We showed our number to an attendant and got in line and trudged along. At the door, we wet our left arm and wiped it with alcohol so that the vaccine would take. There was a Polish boy ahead of me that took his shirt off for what purpose I don't know. We then went to the doctor. He scratched our arm with some object until it was red, but it did not hurt. We then went and had our number stamped.

I went down and ate supper at 6:00 o'clock. We had ham and I ate half when I usually only eat a quarter. They serve gruel at 8:00 o'clock, so I will go down then and eat a little. It is somewhat better with the sea-sickness now. I am not so sick.

March 24, 1910

The boat is sailing smooth now and my appetite is better. For two nights now I have been down in the dining room and listened to music, ate cheese, gruel and rolls. Yesterday a Frenchman sang several songs. I thought it sounded very nice even though I did not understand a single word. The people applauded with vigor. We are expected to be in New York tonight or early in the morning and that will be good. Everyone is tired of the journey.

It would be nice to be home now. They do not celebrate Easter here. We have had the most beautiful weather one could wish for. The waves have not been more than a meter high at any time, and better weather cannot be had. My pillow is so flat that I have my coat under my head.

Eleven a.m.—

The sun is shining, the water is like a mirror, but it is rather cold. The dining room is full of people that are writing in books and some are writing letters. We have been seen by the doctor again and went by him with our hats in our hands. He took some of us out of the line for closer examination. I don't know what could have been wrong with them. At 4:00 o'clock, we are near land and have already seen seagulls.

The cruising speed of the boat was twenty-six and a half knots an hour. The weather continues to be beautiful! Now, at 5:00 p.m., there is a thick fog. We can see only 10 or 15 meters ahead of the boat, and it is just like being inside of a cloud. It is now 10:30 and the fog has lifted and there is a clear moon. The harbor pilot came on board at 9:00 o'clock and the boat is now at anchor in the harbor. We are in New York after five days' travel from Liverpool.

March 25, Good Friday

We were awakened at 5:30 in the morning and went up on deck, formed a line and marched past the "Very Important People" here with our uncovered heads.

When you eat here, you take the risk of being squeezed to death. They are like a band of wolves casting themselves over the food. One has to be made of steel to stand against them.

We went on land at 9:00 a.m. and went to Customs to pay the toll. I had nothing to declare. Later we went to the quarantine station in small boats out on a small island (Ellis Island). When we got on the island, we formed lines and marched forward and there we went through a thorough examination. We went by the first man, who said nothing, and then another that wanted to see our number. We went up some stairs into a room that was divided up into stalls. We then showed our numbers and were shown a stall to go into. A man sat there and looked into our eyes and looked at our eyelids, inside and out, and then to some other matadors that sat at a table.

We had to show them our money. They asked me what I could do. "Paint, I said". I then had to tell them how much money I had, which was $23 and they wrote that down.

Later we went to a big hall to show our papers and got tickets. There was only one other person that was going to travel the same way as me. I don't know who he is, he cannot talk Swedish. I sat on the sofa and waited. All of a sudden, an old man came and got me and the other person. We rode with him in a boat over to the city where he led us to a big house. We went into a room, where I sat and wrote. There are two other people in the room, none of us understand the other. It is terrible! One would not think it is so hard unless you experience it yourself.

There is a train that goes in the air here. It must be electric. I don't see any locomotive. We are on the second floor and can see far out in the distance. There are swarms of cabs and wagons and more.

It is just as warm here as summer back home. Three more men have come here, so now we are six. Of all of us here, I have heard only two that understand each other, maybe they are from Finland. Their dialect is the same. One of us is probably German, it says Hamburg on his travel bag. You can't believe how boring it is with "Babel's confusion"! You have to be quiet as a mouse, no one understands you.

March 26, 1910, 7:00 o'clock

We are now five people in this room and we all speak a different language so no one understands the other person. Myself and another boy about 18 years old share a room. At first, I thought he was from England, but he does not seem to understand the way they talk here, but he does read the newspaper here in New York. Maybe he is from the farm country in England.

I have not slept in such a soft feather bed as I slept in last night. I sank down about 20 inches when I laid down. At 5:30 in the morning an old woman came and knocked on the door and said, "all right". I believe that she meant that we should get up. We got up and went downstairs (there was no bathroom in our room). A woman came and gestured by rubbing her cheeks and showed us a room where there was water to wash up with. We went in and washed up and then went into another room where a man sat and pointed to the kitchen and said "coffee". We went in and there the other men were already eating. Breakfast consisted of coffee, almost raw meat, fried a little and when you cut into it, the blood ran.

Everything is so strange to me—as if I fell out of the sky! I helped an old man on with his coat today. He is completely gray-haired and looks like he is 60 years old. Both women are just as old if not older. The old man is sitting and smoking. I wonder what will happen next?

The street cars here are twice as long as they are back home. There are no overhead wires. Instead there is a rail in the middle of the tracks that powers the train. The streets are full of people and most of them are finely dressed. I have never seen anything that compares. They don't heat with wood here. They use wooden shavings, paper, boxes and old clothes. The stove stands in the middle of the floor with a stove pipe right across the whole room.

March 27, 1910

It is Easter today, but I have not seen any Easter eggs. They came and got the English boy yesterday. The German also left yesterday, so now I have another room companion. I think he is a Frenchman because he showed me a French franc.

We had the same breakfast today as yesterday. The meat was a little more done, but we did not get any Easter eggs. I don't like the food, both the way it is served, or the time we eat. We get food three times a day, 7:00, 12:00 and 5:00 o'clock, then we don't get any more. We get coffee in the morning poured into a big tea cup with the cream already in the cup. The sugar is in the bowl. There are no sugar cubes. The teaspoons are set out in a bowl. The food is served on a dinner plate, and the whole plate is covered with meat. The food that is not eaten is thrown in the garbage or whatever happens to it.

A few slices of bread are served on a plate, and when that is gone, a few more slices are put on, so it is filled several times. It is not the same bread you get back home. A more tasteless bread cannot be found. It is baked in long loaves, looks like wheat bread at home, but just tastes dry. Just think, if we only had a little Swedish bread! For dinner, soup is served first—ten different kinds, and the most that is in them is onions and pepper. Later we get meat and big white potatoes. If you want anything to drink, you get water, so I don't enjoy such a food menu.

I was out and looked at the city for a while. The street I was on was as flat as a floor the whole way. The buildings are so high that you can hardly see the top of them. Along the walls of the buildings, shoe shine boys were busy with their work. They had high chairs that their customers sat on while their shoes were being polished. It is very unpleasant here in my taste. I would not want to live in New York. I wonder how long I will have to stay here. If only I could speak the language!

March 28, 1910, day after Easter

Today is my brother Ludwig's birthday. He is having a much better day today than I am. I was out yesterday afternoon and among other things, saw John Ericcson's statue down by the harbor. I also saw the Statue of Liberty. It stands on an island out in the harbor. There is a light in her hand that can be seen all over the harbor.

The warmth is starting to take effect, the buds on the trees are starting to swell. I think that I have been here long enough. Maybe the meaning is that I won't get any further. This is no enviable lot I have here. I have been here five days now and got the same food every meal except today. I live at 45 Whitehall Street.

March 29, 1910

I was out by the harbor for a while today. There were many people and boats there. There were seven or eight shoeshine boys shining shoes. I let one of them shine my shoes. It cost 5 cents, and they shine like the sun in Karlstad. I bought a dimes worth of bananas and got ten of them. There are many organ grinders, but I don't think they earn much money, but the shoeshine boys, I think, do fine.

I have not seen a full-blooded negro here, but mulattos are probably 10 percent of New York's population from what I can figure out. Three of them are coming now. I don't know who they are. They look like ruffians.

March 30, 1910

The hour of liberation has come! We went with a man to the steamboat office and got our tickets. We each got a long paper that I did not understand more than I wrote down my name and Kingsburg. They then came and picked us up in a horse and carriage and went flying down to the harbor so fast that our knapsacks jumped all over.

Drive, they can in New York! I think it was about a mile to the harbor. We went on board the steamship Commers that will take us to New Orleans.

March 31, 1910

I am now traveling full speed ahead to the tropics. The weather is beautiful, the sun is bright, and the waves are slight, so that the boat shakes more than it rocks. There are only 18 people in third class. There are no private cabins here, but many more in second-class. They all have to sleep in one large cabin. We lay on a thick spread out woven fabric with a straw cushion for pillow and one blanket under and one on top for bedclothes.

We get enough meat to feed a whole company and that is all we get that is worth anything. The coffee and the mutton we get is so poor, that I would rather drink water and even that is tasteless.

April 1, 1910

I have felt so poorly yesterday and today that I could not write. I feel like I have gotten a good beating, I'm so tired that I could hardly get out of bed the whole night, and half a day yesterday and half a day today. You can see that we're coming to a warmer climate. The sun is so hot that they have spread a canvas over the deck so that we are shielded from the sun.

It is now night. When you come up on deck it reminds one of the Midsummer's night in the Nordic North. The air is so tepid and pleasant. The boat is going so smooth you cannot feel it move, almost as if it stood still. There is no wind. It is a real delight to be on deck.

If only the food was good and I had someone to talk to it would be a pleasure cruise, but the way it is, it is as though you were a dog. You hear the others talk, but don't understand a word. If I spoke the language, I could make myself understood. Now it's just as if a dog barks or a cat meows. Speaking of cats, there are four or five here on the boat.

I have never seen dinnerware made of just tin before. The knives are some other metal and so rusty that I can't tell what they are made of.

April 2

I am sitting on the boat's anchor and have my book on the rail writing.

The boat is going so close to land that in the distance you can see the coast like a blue edge. You can even see trees in some places. Just now, we're passing a lighthouse. We have gone by two of them earlier in the day. For a while, we saw two big fish swimming alongside the bow. They were more than a yard long. They swam so close that we saw them the whole time, and once in a while they jumped out of the water. They swam like that for about five minutes, and then disappeared and we did not see them again. Right after, we saw a school of flying fish. Those we only saw for a few minutes. They look something like a swallow, except the wings are shorter and look like the wings of a housefly. The whole fish is about nine inches long. If they did not have wings they would look like a perch.

April 3

The heat is dreadful! It is so warm that you could melt. The nights are not so warm, then it is cool and pleasant. Yesterday I sat up on deck and watched the flying fish. It is absolutely full of them. They fly like birds. The first time I saw them, I thought they were birds. There are masses of jellyfish laying and swimming in the water. One cannot believe how hopeless it feels to see only sky and water. It is as if the boat is standing still in the middle of the ocean. No matter how fast it goes, it is still the same and the same.

April 4, 1910

Now the picture has changed! A River pilot came on board last night at one o'clock to pilot the boat into the Mississippi River. They anchored the boat in the middle of the river. To the right of us is a pretty farm with many buildings. I think they are painted with oil paint and have tile roofs. The trees in New York were bare, but they are not here. Here, they are so bloomed out and green that I was surprised. It is foggy now, so I can't see anything real clear, but I do see red flowers. It will be nice to get away from the sea journey. I had already enough of that in Liverpool.

4 p.m.

At last we are in New Orleans! The boat lifted anchor at eight a.m. and started full speed ahead toward the town, and we got there at two o'clock. It was nice to travel up the river, alongside the banks are small homey houses, completely embedded in the greenery. By each and every house is a pier with one or more boats. You can see many different colors here, black, brown, gray, red, yellow and white. It is so beautiful along the banks that you become charmed.

We were met with a horse and carriage that took us to a station. We waited there until a man came out and got us and took us to some kind of hotel or whatever it was. We will be here for the night. I thought we would leave today, but that was wrong. The two Portuguese and I were the only ones that came here, the others left today. This place is worse than a woodshed. Just plaster on the walls, no windows. If you want some light, you have to open the door.

April 5, 1910

We have to supply our own food. It was too warm to sleep last night and I had only one blanket on me.

11:30 a.m.

I am finally on the train. The individual we stayed with last night charged us. We assumed that it was included in our fare. One of us gave him two dollars and got 30 cents back. As luck would have it, I only had 65 cents, which I gave him. He shook his head when I showed him my empty change purse, but he took what I had. Had he known that I had 23 dollars, he would've wanted that too.

We rode to the station and were there a couple of hours before we could go into one of the coaches. We had to show our tickets before we could go in. These are fine coaches, stuffed sofas upholstered in red. The coaches are as fine as second class at home in Sweden.

April 6th, 1910

The sofas are constructed in such as fashion so that they can be adjusted into many positions to fit your back.

We are going through Louisiana now and it is very pretty with big rail stations and not too far in between them. It has been bright sunshine the whole time. The worst is when you try to sleep. It has been almost impossible in such an uncomfortable place such as this. You are awakened many times when they check the ticket stub in your hat. They have checked mine four times already.

We have now crossed the plains of Texas. It took two days even through the train traveled at a good rate of speed. Nothing grows on the plains except small stunted bushes, but I think there were plenty of animals. I saw a dead calf and a deer along the tracks and here and there a pile of bones from some animal.

April 8, 1910

I am now in Los Angeles, sitting on a sofa in the waiting room, writing. I stopped yesterday because the train was rocking and shaking too much. I even saw some rabbits hopping among the tufts of grass. We rode on a bridge that was at least 200 meters long. I bought a photo of the bridge. We changed trains one time in Texas, with much nicer coaches. We each got a seat that you could use as a bed when you laid down the back rest.

It is dreadful that I cannot speak the language. I can't get a cup of coffee or anything else. Yesterday, I sat and ate my hardtack dry and had nothing else to drink except water. A young boy came and asked me if I was Swedish. He said he thought I was when he saw me eating hardtack. You can't believe how nice that was. It was as if I had met a brother. He went and bought coffee for me in my glass jar. It cost 10 cents. It tasted good, after not having any for more than three weeks. The worst of it was, is that he was going to get off at the next station, so I did not get to talk to him for more than 15 minutes. He had Swedish parents, but was born in America.

When I got to Los Angeles, I sent a telegram to Gulbransen that said I would leave here today. That cost 40 cents. I wonder how soon I will leave? I have shown my ticket 2 times already, but it is not my turn. I hope I don't have to wait too long!

3 o'clock

I have plenty of time to write today. I have to wait until 9 o'clock, that will be 12 hours. That is not very pleasant, but I hope that my journey will soon come to an end. It is not very warm here. I am freezing! I am writing to pass the time otherwise, I have no lust for anything, I can hardly see or hear.

Today we rode through some orange groves. They are pretty trees to see. Some are blooming, some have bright fruit, and some are half ripe. It is unbelievable how the money goes. I have spent two dollars on the train and I don't know what I got for them.

April 10, 1910

I am now in Kingsburg. I left Los Angeles at 11 o'clock on the eighth and arrived here at 11 o'clock on the ninth. That was yesterday. When I got to the station in Kingsburg, there was no one to meet me. I went into the waiting room and wrote down Gulbransen's address and then went outside and showed it to a man. He asked me if I was from Sweden and then took me with him to find Torsten. He was out in town, were we found him in a butik (boutique). Esther was also in town. I rode home with her and now I am finally at my goal.

It is beautiful in Kingsburg. Each night is like a Midsummer's night-- the telegram came the day after I arrived here.

Kingsburg, California, April 14, 1910   A.L

FOREWARD

MY DESTINY AND ADVENTURES

When I was home in Sweden, I often read in the newspapers how dangerous it was to travel to America. Therefore, I thought that I would describe my destiny and experiences here in the "promised land".

Since I have only a regular education, I may not write or spell proper, but hold myself to the truth I can, and I will. I will point out the light and dark side of everything I experience.

I have been in the United States for eight months now as of this writing and can now first write down what I have experienced. Later I will try to write down something at least every week

Kingsburg, California
December 12, 1910

Albrekt Lundquist

BOOK 1

Chapter 2

LIFE IN AMERICA

I arrived in Kingsburg on the **ninth day of April 1910** and stayed with my relatives. I rested for several days and later started to hang wallpaper for my cousin. That took three weeks. Later I got to help with the watering in the orchard. Everywhere there is unusual watering because California does not have much rainfall. The water that they use is melted snow that comes from the high mountain (on some of the mountains the snow never melts away). The water leaks down in canals and from the canals it goes into ditches and from ditches into furloughs between the trees.

I helped with the watering for about one month. It was very trying for me to go out into the 105° heat. You must wear a wide brimmed hat to shade yourself from the sun's burning rays. I didn't have one at first, so I became so sunburned that I peeled most of the skin off of my face.

I helped with clothes washing one day. "In America, there are just as many men that do this work as women". So I rolled up my sleeves. I did not feel anything at first, but later my arms became tender and red, and the next week I could tear off big pieces of skin from them.

I was up one night and watered the alfalfa. "It is like clover and used for fodder". That was a beautiful night! The moon rose as red as blood and from the ditches you could hear the frogs croaking. Everything was like it was wrapped up in a veil. The air was so light and pleasant.

The moon rose higher up. It is now shining in its full brilliance and mirroring itself in the water that runs on the cultivated ground and slowly the water rises until there is enough, then I let it into another route. Now and then the silence is broken by some birds fluttering and chirping.

In the East the horizon is fading more and more. The high mountains sketch themselves like a dark grey cloud bank, but now the highest edge of the cloud bank is golden, the birds are twittering and the sun's radiating ball rises majestically over the mountain tops. The time is 4:30 a.m. and I'm going in and rest. Gulbrand can take over the watering.

I have decided to travel up to the mountains and work in the big forest. I can get my trip paid faster that way, and get myself ready for the trip at the end of May, and have companionship with another Smalander from my home tract that has been in the forest before.

JOURNEY TO THE MOUNTAIN

We rode from home at 4 a.m. in the morning. I was conveyed by a farmer named Bolander and Stolgren, his brother. We rode two in a cart. When we came to Sanger (a little town that was on the way) we stopped and had breakfast. Later we didn't get anything to eat before late afternoon. At last we came to Tollhouse, a small town that lay just below the most torturous hill that we were going up. There we put our horses in a stall and went into the hotel and ate supper. Later we started our trip to "Tollhouse Hill". The way was so steep it rose 1 foot for every 3. You feel it in your breast when you go up such a hill. We could drive only a little each time. We had to rest because the horses became sweaty and overheated. The higher we came, the fresher the air became. You inhaled in one full drag. It was like one thought he could live on air alone.

At last we came up after a three-hour march. It was then dark, but we found an old stall to put our horses in. We ourselves laid out under the bare heavens. I'll never forget! When we woke up after much needed sleep, my eyes fell on a sky high spruce tree and all around us we saw the big forest, mountains and hills. We had breakfast in a cabin not far from there. Later we journeyed to Petterson's Mill, a big sawmill, where we were going to ask for work. We had 6 miles to go (when I say mile I mean an English mile). We came to the mill at 11 a.m. We ate dinner at 12 o'clock. Later Stolgren asked for work for us, which we got. We were to start work 4th of June.

SKOGEN (THE FOREST)

At night, we went and looked up a so-called "cabin" that we were to live in. I swept out the cabin and cleaned it up and carried an old bed that was nailed together of boards that I was going to lay in. For a mattress, I used cedar branches and spruce branches and straw. I laid a mat under me and a blanket on top. We then rested several hours in the fresh forest air. At 5:15 a.m. the alarm went off, and we got up and dressed and went to the cookhouse and ate. The food was beef, potatoes, coffee and biscuits. The biscuits were baked of water, wheat flour and baking powder and served warm. For a Swedish newcomer, coarse rye would have tasted 10 times better. We were to start work at 6 a.m. Stolgren and myself were to chop oak wood to start with. We went up in the forest and attacked a big oak. So then we were to saw and chop the best we could in six hours. Then it was midday.

I have never been so tired as I was that day. I could hardly go home at night. I sat and rested a while, while Stolgren went for water. I heard a rattlesnake in the bushes near me, but I didn't want to disturb my rest even though I knew how dangerous the snake was. Maybe the snake felt sorry for me and let me go.

I couldn't eat the first few days, if it was because of the fresh air or because I was not used to that kind of work, I don't know. I had to chop oak wood for four days, then I had to stack boards that was my job the whole time, except for two weeks when I helped drive lumber in the lumberyard

I worked in the forest for three months and was paid $40 for the first month and $45 for the other months. The last time I had an American for a partner so I then learned a little English. That time the work was not so hard when you get used to it, but the time went so slow.

Since there was no rain, it became dusty when you drive the horses so that when you meet somebody you could hardly see them. The fallen tree stumps and branches became dry as powder. If a fire were to start it would be near to impossible to stop. The only way to try to stop it is to set backfires so that it cannot spread. I went with to put out a big fire. I wrote the whole thing in my book and now will include it here.

FOREST FIRE

Just after midday 10 August, the air suddenly became full of smoke. Big leaf ashes and burnt out sparks fell down on the ground. We thought that there must be some big forest fires somewhere. Towards evening the smoke disappeared and we heard no more.

On August 12, we were awakened by a fierce alarm signal. We got up and went into the cookhouse and ate breakfast which was ready for us. There was a horseback rider asking for more people to help put out a fire that they could not manage. He couldn't get more than 14 men to help out, six Americans, six Swedes, one Norwegian and one-half Indian.

We left home at 5 o'clock and followed the footpath until we came to "Cold Spring" an Indian wigwam. We got there about 7 o'clock and were divided into three. Then we went on our own directions. The three I was with went the furthest. We went about 3 miles uphill and downhill. In some places, it was so charred that I rode down the hills on my shovel. We set back fires three or 4 miles from the fire in the dry grass. When we were there and set fires close to 2 o'clock, the forest ranger came with food for us which was good under the circumstances. I ate three hard-boiled green cooked eggs and was surprised that I didn't become sick from them. Later we went back to the other five firefighters. The fire had overtaken them when we came and jumped over their backfire, so there was nothing to do but run for your burning life. With the fire at our heels, we had to go through almost impassable brush and woods in some places that was so tight that I had to take my spade in hand and crawl on all fours until we came to a sheltered place. How it murmured, sparked and crackled in the trees! The other men didn't have food until 5 o'clock in the afternoon, a period of 12 hours, and still worked the whole time. It was almost impossible to get water, and when you did, it was warm. Towards night we went a few miles further away, and set backfires in the grass. It was a beautiful spectacle to see the fire all over in the dark night. It looked like a burning ribbon and garlands in the grass and like big torches up on the summit. When we had burnt up all the grass there was, it was after 11 o'clock at night. Then we ate up all the food we had left.

Later we went to Cold Springs and took up night quarters. There was a little block house on the hill. There lived a pair of cow herders, and there we got blankets to cover ourselves. I laid outside. There was a Norwegian that laid with his hat and big long gloves with cuffs on them the whole night. When we got up in the morning my comrades and I had lain on a sticker hill with three big stones under us, but that, we didn't feel. That's how tired we were.

We got up at 7 o'clock and had a little food and then went out and set some more backfires. When we saw the way, we had gone the night before, I was surprised that we could go there.

The way was like a stone pile, almost vertical in some places. Later we left and set fires until 5 o'clock. Then we left and went home and got there about 6:30 p.m. we went by way of the Indian's main roadway. That was miserable to see, in some places it went straight up so that you had to go on both your hands and feet. We went up one hill so long and steep and in spite of the cold, we were soaked with sweat when we came to the top. One of us, the strongest breasted person, would pant like a dog after he went 20 or 30 steps. The fire was not completely under control when we went home, but there was no danger. Rattlesnakes and other animals probably had a reminder about mortality. We saw just one snake that crawled out from under a brush pile, but we did not kill it. We were paid $6.75 for our work from the government.

FALL IN CALIFORNIA

We quit work in the forest September 17th and hired an American to drive us to Fresno. We left Petterson's Mill on Sunday afternoon and came to Fresno on Monday afternoon. That is a beautiful town, somewhat bigger than Jonkoping in my homeland. We were in Fresno about a day and later took the train to Kingsburg. I stayed a while with my relatives and did various jobs, picked grapes and at the last worked as a Master Painter a few weeks. I am now in the employ of Bromarks Company in Kingsburg. They paint so much different here than they do in Sweden so that I will get only $2.00 a day to start with. We haven't worked for three days now because it is so foggy in the air that we cannot paint. I have rented a room here in town. It cost $1.25 a week. I prepare my own food. It is too expensive to eat in the boarding house when you don't work every day.

December 17, 1910

It is Saturday afternoon. I have just enjoyed a good cup of coffee that I cooked myself in the loneliness of my room. It is now just one week before Christmas and here it is green everywhere on the ground. Seeds germinate the whole winter. It is like the month of September in Sweden. This week we have only worked two days and I have 6 miles to go to work but they have fine bicycle paths here in the winter. In the summer, you almost get fastened to the oil that they spray on them.

Since I gave this the title "Fall in California", then I should describe Fall here. It is not the same as in Sweden. The Fall months are September, October and November. In September, the temperature can go up to 105° for several days and never lower than 68° and almost never so low that the water freezes.

At the end of May and beginning of June they start to harvest apricots, the end of July they harvest peaches and almost the whole month of August. The end of August the vineyards have their first harvest which is dried for raisins. Later the end of September, they pick wine grapes. They pick them into large crates and take them to the winery and make alcohol from them and all sorts of wines.

The cost of living is higher in California than in the other states in the union. You can't get room and board for less than $3.50 a week any place. You can get better pay for your work. A farmhand gets $.35-$.40 an hour here in this country. The time is 5:30 PM and the sun is going down. I am going to shave now.

December 26, 1910

Today is the day after Christmas for us Swedes, but Americans celebrate Christmas today. If a holiday comes on a Sunday, then they celebrate it on a Monday instead. The day after Christmas is not celebrated in America. This is my first Christmas in

California. There is a difference between Christmas here and in Sweden. I was with my relatives Christmas Eve. We had it very pleasant the whole evening. All of the food was traditional Swedish, Swedish sausage, hardtack, limpa, presyltta, lutefisk and Christmas porridge. The porridge was appetizing and also had an almond in it. My thoughts went over the Atlantic to my homeland. This was the first Christmas I was away from my home. At 5 o'clock they celebrate Christmas Eve in the churches in Kingsburg. I came to the Swedish Lutheran Church at 5:05 p.m. and it was already full of people so that there was no place to sit, so I was there for only half an hour. I later went to the Baptist Church. There it was not so full so there was a place to sit. They had a Christmas tree in the church with burning candles on it. There was a beautiful decorated tree in the Lutheran Church. Exactly a Swedish tree, that in the other church they had just a small fir. One would think that out of six churches in an American community, one would be Swedish and the others English, but here it is the other way around. You can talk Swedish to anyone so this is not a good place to learn the English language. I think it is strange that a mass of Swedes in a foreign land can't have the same religious beliefs without having five different places to hear God's Word. I forgot to mention that they do not have Mass the way they do in Sweden. It would be more impressive if they had that.

I have never ridden a bicycle to Christmas Eve until this year. Here it is like summer all year, so it is not like Christmas when you don't see snow and when it is not cold. The rain seldom falls in the winter and never in the summer, but it can be foggy, so thick that you can only see a stone's throw in front of you, and so cold that it goes right through your bones and marrow. I have written in chapters before, but that I can't do now because I don't know what will happen faster than the time goes. I have worked 4 days last week and will likely work the same this week.

January 7, 1911

I am out of work now. I hope to have some work soon, at least for a couple weeks. Here it is beautiful weather every day, so that you are anxious to have a little rain. It is so warm in the middle of the day that it is like summer home in Sweden. I know I have worked outside this time of the year before, but this week I worked only three days with outside painting. Now there is no work at all in Kingsburg and I believe there is hardly any in the whole state of California. In the big towns like San Francisco, Los Angeles, Sacramento and Oakland, there is no work either now, but I hope there will be by Spring, then I will leave here, for in Kingsburg one must be a farmer to get work every day.

March 7, 1911

I am now back with Miss Lind. I have lived with Gulbrand a few months, so I could not write in my daybook until now, good that I have it here. I got a job right away the last time I wrote in my daybook. I painted a whole house inside in 10 days, I got $20 for that work. Later I hung wallpaper for $10, then, I painted for Bromark for $10, but you can't become rich when you don't earn more than $40 in two months' time. Now I have something in sight to be a laborer again. To think with that type of work I can earn $100 over three months' time, but to labor in my own trade, I have only earned enough for room and board.

March 7, 1911

It has been so rainy you could not work even if you had work, but I have not had any. I, in seven months have not been able to earn more than enough for food. Me, who thought I would make money like grass! I have so much to write about, but I have no interest in anything. The time goes slow, as if you were in jail and you can't go out because the streets are like a clay gruel.

March 10, 1911

I asked the man that makes sidewalks for work today, but he can't do anything until the rain stops. One can be so tired of this life you want to chuck it all. Go day in and day out on the sidewalk and not look at another person the face as if you did something wrong-- it can drive you out of your mind!

March 13

Now the work sun has begun to shine on me and that it has done so effectively that I am so tired that my limbs feel like they are broken apart. I have a job as a mortar carrier. Today we made mortar and eight hours a day. It is beautiful weather now, so I hope that I can soon get a paintbrush in my hand again. I get $2.25 a day for this work, but I would much rather paint, even if I got only one dollar a day.

March 16, 1911

I am dead tired! It aches in every limb. My job is to haul bricks in a wheelbarrow. I have to wheel them up a gangplank. I have no money and hardly any skin on my hands. I have not been paid from Bromark for the last paint job and it is now three weeks since we finished it.

The time is now 9:30 p.m. and I am going to bed. Now I will see if I can do anything tomorrow. Maybe I won't be able to get up?

March 19,1911

I was very tired Friday morning, but somehow, I got up anyway. I got my money from Bromark Friday afternoon and then I quit Stone that night. Saturday, I had a free day and yesterday I chopped wood and got $2.25 for the day. We were two that chopped, me and another painter. I have nothing to do today, and today is like a Spring day in Sweden. The grass is green and the buds are opening upon the trees and a mist of rain is falling. When you go outside you can almost hear a cuckoo bird, but that I won't hear until I come to the "Land of the Midnight Sun"

March 27, 1911

Now it is Spring in California. Everything is green. The trees, like the firs and cedars, are getting new green needles and it is warm in the air. Yesterday, it was so warm that you sweated. I worked five days last week and this week I don't know if I will have anything to do. I am waiting for an answer on an ad that I put in the Swedish paper, but I don't think anyone has work for a painter now.

April 5, 1911

I have had painting jobs for a few weeks now and I think there will be more in the future. It has been very warm for a few days. One day it was 91°F and it never gets that warm in Sweden. I am still my own cook and that is really good. There is a theater here in Kingsburg, so I think I will go there tonight.

April 17

Today is the day after Easter, yesterday I ate Easter eggs. I have quit my employment with Bromark now, as I do not think that I have any idea to stay in Kingsburg. You can have it good here, but you can neither earn money or learn to talk English. Maybe I made a mistake to quit here, but if I follow my own impulse-- if it goes well I have no one to thank and if it doesn't, I have no one to blame.

April 25, 1911

Now life has changed! Vitas Stolgren and I traveled from Kingsburg Wednesday morning and came to Fresno and planned to stay two hours, but came too late and missed the train so we stayed six hours. We came to Stockton 8 o'clock at night and stayed overnight. Stockton is a big fine town and one of the biggest buildings is the Madhouse. Here they send all the insane people from the whole state. The building is surrounded by a beautiful park. We stayed there an hour, then we continued our journey to Sacramento, the state capital. We came there at noontime and left at midnight. We saw the capital in Sacramento. That is a fine building that is surrounded by a park, one of the most beautiful I've ever seen. We sat in the park a few hours and then rode the trolley through the whole town. Our goal was the Mommont Gold Mine! A man told us that we could earn $75 a month and room and board for eight hours of work, so it was not with the worst expectations we left Sacramento at night, but does it always go the way you expect? We came to the Kennet Train Station at 8 o'clock in the morning and then walked to the mine. The mine was at the top of a high mountain 4 miles high, so when we went up that high with our knapsacks, we were very tired. I have seen many ugly places in my life but never a place as ugly as Mommont *Copper* Mine (it was not a gold mine as we thought). Everything was red Earth and burned up, and here and there stood a withered tree. Everything had a touch of death. Our path went continually upward.

Once in a while we met an Italian or "Dago" as they call them here. All southern Europeans go by that name here. When we finally came up to the mine, it looked so terrible that no one in their right mind would want to work there. The pay was $2.75 a day and $.75 a day for food. Eight hours work time, every other day and every other week work. You had to have your own bed clothes with you. You couldn't buy anything up here if you didn't have it with you so you did without.

So now that the "air castle" fell down, we packed up and got the hell down as fast as we could! It was hard work to get up the mountain but so much worse to go down. When we finally got down, our legs were so sore that we could hardly walk. We stayed in Kennet one night, and then headed up to Shasta Springs. There we got off the train and drank water. There are two kinds of water here, sulfur and soda. Both kinds come from a high cliff. You could drink as much as you wanted and for free. Shasta water is good for your health. We set our course for a little town called Sisson and then from there to McCloud, a big sawmill. We came here on Saturday afternoon and left today, Tuesday. We asked five bosses for work today, but did not get any. Yesterday two Greeks were shot with a revolver. One got a bullet through his neck and is most likely dead as I write this. The other got shot through his arm and will survive. The one that shot them has not been found or why he shot them is not known.

Now we are back in Sisson! I asked a painter for work today and he said he wanted to talk to me tonight and now it is well into the night and I still haven't seen any painter. We are staying in Sisson tonight, and in the morning, we are thinking of going to another sawmill further North. If we don't work soon, then I don't know how it is going to go. In McCloud, there are about 2000 workers there and almost 200 Greeks and 100 Italians that are waiting for work. This town is in a valley with high snow mountains around it. The highest is Mount Shasta with an elevation of 14,444 feet above sea level.

April 28, 1911

We went to another sawmill on Wednesday and we were there two days and thought we would get work, but there were people all over. They are building a railroad in Oregon. People that want to go there get free travel from Sacramento, Los Angeles and San Francisco and get paid $1.75 to $2.40 a day. Many of them take advantage of the free ride and when they get there, they look for work in the big sawmill too. That is the reason it is so hard to find work here. When we were in Weed, we slept on the floor in a big cabin but at least there was heat so we didn't have to freeze. There was a young boy that shot opium into his arms so that he could sleep and have lively dreams. He slept night and day. The following night we slept in a hotel.

When we left there, we saw the opium boy laying in a bed wrapped in slumber. His face was wax gold and he looked more dead than alive. We walked to Sisson today. It is a 12 mile walk. We have rented a room here for the night and are thinking to go back to McCloud in the morning. If we can't get any work here, then I don't know what we will do. We are going to leave our knapsacks here. When you walk it is enough of an effort to go free and easy. I'm going to leave my book in my knapsack and won't write anymore until I have found work.

May 1, 1911

Now I had better write again for now I have found work. We left our knapsacks in the saloon and since we did not have much money left, we walked. In some places we took shortcuts so it was more likely 16 miles to McCloud the way we went. In some places, we went through tangled brush that looked like Hawthorne. When we got there, we were promised work in a box factory. We were to work at night, starting at 7 p.m. and quit at 6 a.m. Now that we had work, we wanted our knapsacks with us, so I had to go to Sisson to get them. I thought I would ride the train home. When I got to Sisson, I learned that the train would not go back until the day after, so I had nothing else to do but go back to McCloud at night or the day after. A room for the night cost $.50 and the train cost $1.00, so I thought that I could just as well go at night as the day since I did not have enough money for a room. I banded the knapsacks together and started my journey. I went the same way as before through the Hawthorne bushes. It was hard to go free and easy, so you can imagine how it was to go with a heavy knapsack. Back home in Sweden they would not understand what a journey like that was. When I finally came up to the road it was so dark so that I could not take any shortcuts and had to go the entire 18 miles with my heavy knapsacks, dead tired and alone through the dark woods. I likened my journey many times with "Kristen's Journey" before he was free of his burden. After a six-hour march, I finally got home. Now I am going to rest a while and later I'm going to work the whole night.

I have now been here three nights, so I can write what I think of it. *I don't like it!* My job is to take boards from a small saw that goes with such a speed that you would think work could not go that fast. I have to take away three or four boards a second. Each worker has a number. Mine is 609. This number is fastened to a ring around the clock. By each number is a hole and there you punch your number, morning and night. If you forget to do that, you don't get paid for your time. Most of the workers here are Greek or Italian. They talk very little English. The one that operates the saw that I work on asked me what time it was in his own language.

It is very cool down here at night, so that you don't even keep warm while working. The worst of it is for me that I can't sleep during the day. Today I couldn't sleep more than a few hours. We got $2.00 a night for work and the room and board is $23 a month, and both are terrible and then you have to pay one dollar to the hospital there, so you have only $1.00 a day for work. That is the worst earnings I have had since I came here. It is tiresome to complain, but as I said before, that I would tell the truth. I won't stay here longer than I can earn $4.00 or $5.00 and then go back for work somewhere else. That is how it is when you hear of gold mines and easy money. They are only soap bubbles that break apart into the tiniest specks.

I have worked in the box factory for five and half nights now and that will be all. That Greek had easy boards to saw this morning, where he could saw with great speed, so he thought he would torture me and saw as fast as he could. I couldn't take away half of what he sawed and soon there was a big pile on the floor, and it grew bigger than my patience. I went home and laid down.

I was out today and looked for work and found work in the lumberyard. I get $2.35 a day and work during the day, so that was good that the pile of boards grew bigger than my patience. There is a Swedish boss and he would rather have Scandinavians to work with there. He pays them $.25 a day more than "Dagos".

May 10, 1911

We are thinking of quitting here now we cannot earn any money here in this cold hole. You just catch cold here. I have had a bad cold and have been able to work only one day on my new job. We are thinking of going to the copper mines and sending our knapsacks ahead.

May 18

It's been a long time since I wrote in my daybook. I didn't write because I didn't see it. Now I have at last come to a place where I think I will stay and be satisfied with. We sent our knapsacks to Kennett ahead of us, and they have been there a whole month, so I could not write anything in my daybook, but I wrote everything down in my notebook.

We quit in McCloud the 10th of May. Stolgren had to pay his taxes, so he only had $.75 left, but I had $2.90 left. That was not very much money to set out with, but we had to go. We walked to Sisson and hired a room for the night. Later we walked to Dunsmuir. That was 8 miles. We passed Shasta Springs on the way, and since we were not on the train we had time to stop and freshen up with the wells fizzing soda water. There are four or five wells. There is clear water, sulfur and soda water.

Shasta Springs lies at the foot of a high mountain. The first well is Clear Spring and then you come to Moss Spring, and it is so close to the railroad, you come to the soda well, and further down in the Valley is the Sacramento River with its wild rush between the cliffs and the rocks.

The well I have just talked about comes from deep in the earth. In some places, it throws a stream of water as high as 30 or 40 feet high. Shasta water is good for the health and is bottled and sent all over. Shasta Springs is the most beautiful I have seen so far in California, but our empty wallets tell us that we can't stay long here by this masterwork of nature. We each took a bottle of water and continued our wandering to Dunsmuir.

We came there in the evening and since we didn't have much money we did like the other tramps and rode a freight train. Our boxcar was loaded with timber. We crawled in among the timbers so as not to be seen, but one of the brakeman saw us anyway. So, when we went a way he came shining a lantern and wanted $.50 from each of us, or else he would throw us off, so we paid and rode as freight. When we got to Kennett we went into a restaurant and had coffee, later we slept overnight in the train station. In the morning, we went up to the mine and asked for work, but got none. We got two meals for free. We had nothing else to do but go to another mine that was 6 or 7 miles from there. We followed the path that went outside of a high hill that was full of small stones and so steep that you had to hold in the bushes and tree roots so that you would not go down faster than you wanted to. At last we got down, but then there was nothing but rags left of my shoes.

We walked until we came to Uncle Sam's Goldmine. Here and there we saw a single digger car between the cliffs. We were at the place where earlier, gold was dug up in masses and the blood flowed, but now there are not so many gold diggers. They are mostly copper mines. We got to Uncle Sam's but got no work. We then went to BalaKollala Copper Mines. We got there at night and with luck we got a room that we slept in. There were no bedclothes, so we laid with one mattress under and one on top of us so that was just as good. We get two meals and stayed two nights and then we had to leave or starve to death, for we didn't get any work. We went back to Mommoth, came too late for lunch, so we had nothing to eat until supper at 5 o'clock. We had been without food for 31 hours. We didn't get any work this time either, so we had to leave and go to Anderson. There we could get work on a canal that they were going to dig.

We went from Mommoth to Redding. We got there at midnight and found an empty railroad car that we slept in overnight. Later we went to Anderson and went into the office and there we got work and were to start in the morning. We slept in a hay barn for the night and rode out to the job the next morning. It was 15 miles to the job and we had to pay $1.75

for the ride. When we got to the job in Anderson, we had $.15 left.

Our work was with a steam shovel. We got two dollars a day and paid $5.25 a week for the worst food I've seen in my whole life. We slept in a tent, but I was glad that we did not have to starve. Today is Sunday and we worked half a day today and half a day yesterday. No morning has ever gone as slow as this day. We stood there and chopped and shoveled while the boss (an old red-haired Irish man) sat on a stone right by me with a pipe in his mouth and watched. He looked like a big bear and sat and yelped if something didn't go the way he wanted. (What date that was I don't know) I couldn't sleep today because of the heat. It is so hot that you had to lay under the house to get any sleep. The flies here are massive. The butter melts in the heat and the flies are drowning all over in the food. They are Chinese that prepare the food. They are dirty and ugly when they go here and set out the food, you lose your appetite just to look at them. I am completely ruined in my stomach from the poor food. We worked hard last night and I got hit in the head from a big stone. I lost my pocket watch when we ate supper last night. It was a fine watch that I had paid nine dollars for.

May 30, 1911

Now I believe I that we won't stay here more than two more nights. I am almost certain that the boy that sits across from me at the table is the one that stole my watch. He is a Mexican.

May 31

We quit here today. I had $12 coming and only got

$4.00. I had to pay $6.00 in taxes and then I forgot to write down my number one night, so I worked one night for nothing. It is awful annoying to be forced to talk English and not be understood. I explained the best that I could without results. Vitas Stolgren was also in the office and argued with them. He could talk English just as good as Swedish, but they would not admit that they did wrong. It was with everything but good feelings that I left there. It looked like all my luck had gone, work one night for nothing, my watch stolen, pay six dollars in taxes and forced to buy a pair of shoes and so on. Stolgren had $12, so it was with some comfort that we got to ride with a driver to Anderson. We slept there the night in a hay barn and then we went to Cottonwood. That was a 6-mile trip. Our thoughts were to hop a freight train to Sacramento. One came that night, but then we were on one side and our knapsacks were on the other, so I had to go between the cars and get our knapsacks. Vitas Stolgren was to wait until I got back. When I got back I didn't see any Stolgren so then I could not get on. I thought that Stolgren didn't get on either when he didn't see me, but however it was, he got on and I was left alone. Now it looks like all hope was out for me, but maybe it was good that it happened the way that it did.

I found an empty baggage car and went in, and there was already a regular tramp in there. He was going out to the ditch the next morning, and since I had nothing to do I followed along. Just as we went to sleep, the baggage car was hooked up to a train, and we would have gone back up North if we had not woken up and hopped off. Now we had to sleep under the bare sky. In the morning, we went and bought bacon and bread and cooked coffee and fried bacon and then we ate with a good appetite.

Now I will write up when I wrote in my notebook. I bought a pair of shoes for $3.50 and now I am alone except for a tramp. It is not so good for me, but one must not lose courage. We took our packs on our backs and walked the railroad tracks to the ditch again, but destiny decided that I would not work in that ditch again where I tortured myself for 14 days for four dollars.

We met a farmer who asked us if we wanted to help stack hay for one dollar a day and food. We went with him home and got there Friday night. Here you got the best food you could wish for, but we had to sleep in the hayloft. The first thing we were to do was saw wood. We went out in the woods to a pine that we were to cut down and cut up the stump and then got home at 9 o'clock. My comrade thought that it was too much work to cut down a tree in two hours. He wanted three hours to do that. It could be done in a half hour, but the farmer said we could leave right away. The tramp left, but I wanted to stay if he would have me. I chopped down some bushes to start with, then I drove the horses with the hay rake and raked hay until the mid-day. This is a German farmer that I am with. He has two sons and a daughter of 16 or 17. I am so content here that I will don't miss anything except my watch.

June 6

I have never seen anyone that was so anxious for a man to have good food as this German. Tonight, he is going to write to Kennett for my knapsack. I stayed with this German farmer almost 2 weeks. It was so hot at times that the sweat just dropped off of you, and to work in the hay when you are our sweaty is not easy. When we were done with the hay the German, (His name is George Scharsel). He telephoned up to a sawmill and asked for work for me which I got. I rode on a stagecoach out to the town of Shingle Town. That was 5 miles. Later I rode the 10 miles to the sawmill. Since I didn't have my knapsack with me, Scharsel was going down to Cottonwood and got it and then took it here to the forest where he has another farm and then I will walk there to get it. It is 5 miles to his farm.

The man I rode up here with is a German that worked here last year. He is going to ask for work here again. We got here at 10 o'clock at night and slept outside. We got up at 5:30 a.m. and had breakfast. I didn't have to ask for work. As soon as the boss saw me, he asked me if I wanted to start work right away, but I didn't want to start until after noon. I had to find a cabin so that I would not have to sleep outside. I have worked here a day and a half now. My job is to drive boards and planks to the lumberyard. Here the food is good, the best you can think. We work 11 hours a day. A worker came up here yesterday and had my knapsack. His father was German and his mother is Danish but he could not speak Danish. I am the only one that speaks Swedish here. Now I am starting to have it a little nice again. This is a good place, cool and pleasant, and you can make money, so I will probably stay here until fall.

June 25

If my memory is right, today is Midsummer, but they don't celebrate Midsummer here, they celebrate Fourth of July.

I feel a little gloomy once in a while. They are all Uncle Sam's sons and if I am to talk to anyone I have to talk English and that is not so easy when I have been here only one year. Here is the right place to learn the language, and I think by fall I will be able to speak and write well. In order to have the right dialect you have to be born in this country

I am in the right place now! I can earn money fast, learn the language fast and the food is good and you don't have to work harder than you can tolerate. There is no boss in back of you all the time and you do not have to be "numbered" and best of all, is the cool clean air of the forest that you have to put some value on. Just below my window they are engaged in the national pastime of playing ball. It is probably the only sport or play that they know of in America. I think it falls into childishness
and can't find any interest in it.

July 5, 1911

Yesterday was the USA's biggest holiday and that holiday was so big that we didn't work today either. They started to celebrate Saturday night and will continue on until the early morning. Some of the workers have gone to their homes but I have to go too far to go to mine, so I have to stay here.

July 16

I should write in my book but when you stay in one place there is much to write about. It is quite warm up here. The sunshine is just as warm up here as it is down in the flat land, but the wind blows and it is a cool wind and it cools off the air. Today the wind is calm.

Hair and whiskers grow fast when it is warm. The whiskers I can take care of, but I can't cut my hair. There are many here that can cut hair, but none of them have anything to clip with, so here you have to have your own scissors when you go to the barber.

So that my hair doesn't grow as long as Absalom I have to inconvenience myself and walk 11 1/2 miles to Shingletown and buy a pair of scissors, but there was not a pair to be had. As luck would have it, I met the mailman and asked him to buy me a pair in Cottonwood. It costs $1.50 but then I got a pair of scissors *and* my hair clipped.

August 6

It is Sunday night. The moon's pale shimmer filters through the tall pine green needles down on me as I sit in my solitude with the candle's fluttering illumination. Through the broken window I hear the melodic tones of a violin. It is like a bit of poetry and is broken off by the alarm that calls us to work at 5:15 a.m. every morning. I don't want to write anymore tonight, so I can end this in a poetic mood-- poetry I can write the next time.

I get the Swedish American newspaper every Tuesday. It is the only diversion I have.

August 13

Now it is Sunday night again. I was just in and had dinner. Last night the dining room was converted into a dance hall. I was there for a while and watched. They had fine music, violin and guitar and skillful players. They do not dance here as they do in Sweden. In Sweden, they dance much faster so that the dance becomes work and the dancers become sweaty. Here they go quietly and glide softly to the violins lonesome caressing tones and it is a pleasure just to watch. The women are dressed in white with bracelets and necklaces and rings. They look uncommonly beautiful, all of them, so I wondered if it was really beauty, or if they know that their clothes bought out their beauty in its full appearance.

Masculine partners were not so finely clothed. It was only their solid gold watch chains that were noteworthy. Here it is just the women that should be finely dressed, "women are the creators crown" and I think that the women of this country know that. There is music in the dining room this afternoon. They do everything they can to keep up the pleasantness. Sunday when I wrote, I thought I would write poetry the next time, but that will not be this time either.

August 25

It is Friday night. I have read through my newspaper and now there is nothing else to do but write in my daybook. (Maybe I should call it a weekly or monthly book). There are 40 workers in the sawmill. Is owned by the three Thatcher Brothers and a brother-in-law by the name of Knapp. The last name sounds Swedish and probably is. I saw a Swedish paper addressed to him, but I never heard him talk Swedish. Knapp is the "top 10 in the chicken coop". He sits in the office most of the time and is dressed like a worker. The work is easy; you can rest a half hour if you want.

I will now try to describe how a sawmill looks here in California. The trees are cut down in the forest and cut up into logs and then lashed to a drag line and pulled by steam engine to where you want them. They are then loaded onto big wagons and taken to the sawmill. All is done with the steam engine. The logs are 1 to 2 m in length, some are only 1 foot too. When you are going to saw a log, you put a line around it and roll it up on a rail that goes back and forth into the blade as fast as you want by pulling on a handle. To pull in the handle is the sawers job (you do not have to touch them with your hands like you do in Sweden on a small saw). I have never seen a big saw there. At the same time, he signals to the one on the rail with his fingers as to how thick the boards are to be, and then he moves a log forward by turning a screw.

When the boards are sawn they must pass on iron rollers into an elevator and be raised up to a platform. A man up there loads them onto rollers and then my partner and I moved them out into the lumberyard. The rails are set so that the rollers almost go by themselves. The boards are then stacked into different piles according to quality. It is easy to stack the boards when you take them from high up in the air and put them in a pile. They use two saw blades that meet in the center. The saw blade teeth are designed so that when they are worn out, you just take them out and put new ones in. That was a little bit about a little saw mill, but with a big one it does not go the same way. For example, in McCloud the logs come onto a dam, and are taken up to an elevator that takes them to the saw. The saw is a bandsaw that has teeth on both edges so that every time a log passes, it cuts off a board. The operator sits on a stool and has four or five handles to pull on. So, the machines do all the work. The boards are taken up by an elevator to a big table and they can come so fast that it takes 20 minutes to load them onto rollers and that's how it works in a big sawmill here in the United States

August 29

Now the work here is done. I got $104.70. Now I don't think I will have to go on the bum so soon. I am going to walk to Shingletown and then take a stagecoach to Cottonwood and then later to Oakland.

Now I am in Oakland. This is a big and beautiful city. I got lost as soon as I got here but asked directions and got back on the right way. I went into a big fine hotel and got a room. The man that owns the hotel is a genuine Smalander from Jonkoping. As soon as I opened my mouth he heard that I was Swedish and then I could at least talk Swedish again. I have a room in this hotel for $.25 a day.

September 15

Much has happened since I last wrote in my daybook and now I will write about that. I soon found out that there was no reason to stay in Oakland because there was no work, so I bought a ticket to Kingsburg. I got onto the wrong train and came to Frisco instead of Fresno. I did not plan on going to San Francisco and when you do not have a guide, you do not see so much. Now that I was on the train, I thought "let the roll go".

So now I am in Frisco. This is a big time. It is hilly all over-- if it was because of the earthquake or was like that before, I don't know. I was in the Golden Gate Park. That is the finest park I have ever seen. It is 6 miles long. At the entrance of the park is a statue of Columbus. They have bears, deer, buffalo and many other types of animals in big cages. The temperature in Frisco and Oakland seldom goes over 75°F.

I had an automobile ride to Golden Gate Park and I thought I had to pay a dollar or so, but I had no smaller money than a $10 gold piece and I had to pay that for the ride. I was badly robbed, but there is nothing to do and I will do better next time.

I went to Kingsburg and got a job from Gundersen right away. I stayed with my cousin Gulbrand Nelson a week. Later I was to start work and now we are in full swing. We are painting a high school that is about 70 miles north of Kingsburg. It is the town of Dos Palos. There is just a Swedish boss here from Smaland, and if you travel to the end of the earth, you will meet a Smalander. This is a big building that we are painting. The contractor is getting $1600 for the job. We are painting the roof now. We have already painted the high tower and the scaffolding we used was so poor that you could say that our lives hung in a thread. Had you fallen down from such a height your body would be a bloody mess. As luck would have it, the scaffolding held up and we got back down on the ground with our skin intact. We pay $24 a month for room and board, the food we get is mostly meat, but that is American food. I would rather prepare my own meals then eat here.

I have now been here three weeks and it is like a dance when you can work in your own trade, but now we will have to go back to Kingsburg again, because the carpenters are not done and we have nothing to do. The first Sunday I was there we painted a bank, the contractor and myself. I got $5.50 for 11 hours. I have never earned that much money in one day before. The other Sunday we went to a hot spring about 35 miles from here. We rode in the car from here at 5 o'clock and got there about 6:30. I have never seen a hot spring before so that was something new for me. The water was 140°F so that was pretty hot to bathe in, but when it came into the pool it had cooled off a little, and when you got in you could stand it about 10 minutes. It is also helpful to drink. The water does not taste so bad warm. I drank three or 4 cups.

The painting contractor hasn't been here until today. He came last night and left today at noon. Most likely we will go home on Saturday then I don't know if I will have work or not. The trouble is, that, when you have a building to paint, it has to be done as fast as possible and in between you have nothing to do. I think I would like to have a farm.

October 9, 1911

I have been here for four weeks and now my employment is done. There is only work for the older painters and so we three new ones were laid off yesterday. I got $3.25 a day for nine hours work and paid $1.00 a day in the hotel for room and board.

Herbert Nelson and I are going back to Kingsburg. We didn't have such a long job, but we had a good boss to work for. I worked a month now and had easy work, short hours and good pay. So, it is the same here as in Sweden, for hard work you get the least pay and the other way around.

It is now the end of this book and when it is finished I will start another. I don't know if I will let others read this, it is showing my whole life in the USA, but if others read this or not the truth will be written.

At last----I think I did a wise thing in coming

here----and time will tell.

Dos Palos
October 9, 1911
Albrekt Lundquist

END OF BOOK 1

BOOK 2

January 18, 1912

Kingsburg, California, Miss Lind's place

I am now so lonesome that I can't think of anything else to do but write.

When I came back from Dos Palos, I stayed for two weeks with Guldbrand. Later I moved to Kingsburg, worked for my old boss one month and moved up to Cottonwood again to paint his new house. I was there for five weeks and worked 22 days. I will get $30 for my work.

I am in Kingsburg again, and there is nothing here to lay my hands on. It is so lonesome and gloomy to be lazy that you are disgusted with everything.

I can read English and speak fairly well now but in Kingsburg it isn't often you have to use your knowledge in the English language.

February 22, 1912

It is a long time since I wrote in my daybook, but now it will be. We moved from Miss Lind's place a month ago and rented a little house for $4 a month. We are four of us that live here. It is 2 miles north of town. Here the time goes fast and is not boring. I'm staying home today and cooking beans for supper for when Knut and Carl come home. They are out pruning grapevines. Almond and apricot trees are in full bloom and next week the pears will start. You can hardly find enough work here in the winter to earn enough for food. I took a job to paint a house inside for $35. In a few months, all of us will probably go back up in the forest.

March 6, 1912

Today is Easter Saturday, but it looks like they don't do like they do in Sweden and they don't celebrate Easter either in this land. The lilacs and tulips are in full bloom now, and it's so hot during the day that you could melt. It is more like midsummer than Easter. It is the most beautiful now in Fresno County, green all over, but it will soon be brown from the lack of water. We won't have any rain for the next six or seven months.

You would think that when you have only fruit trees and grapevines that you would not have to work all year, but that is not so. After the harvesting is done, the trees have to be pruned, and that lasts until February. Later the branches are gathered together, and in the Spring a machine comes in chops up the branches into a mulch, so that you get some benefit from the branches you must clip off. Then you have to plow, cover the dirt around the trees, harrow, water and harrow again. When two weeks have gone by it is time to water and harrow and water again. Later it is time to harvest the apricots, and then the pears and the last are the grapes. That way the farmer works the year-round. Alfalfa is used for fodder, that is like clover. You do not need too much to feed a team of horses and you do not have to fertilize here. After the alfalfa is cut all you have to do is water as much as it needs. The rest is up to the good soil and California's glowing sun. There are no stones in the ground here it looks like fine sand.

April 28, 1912

I have been in the forest one week now with the same sawmill I was in a year ago. Most of us here are Swedes. It snows often here now. It is snowing so much here now that we can't work. This is a strange land. It is snowing so heavy that you would think that you are seeing a real beautiful snowfall in Sweden.

May 20, 1912

It is Monday night, and tomorrow night I will have been here one month. I also had to pay my taxes. It is $4 a year and you cannot escape it. The person that collects the taxes goes to the office and gets all the names of all the workers. If a man is under 21 and over 60 he does not have to pay. If a man is under 21 and looks older, he then has to swear to the fact that he is too young. When you get your pay, the taxes are taken off and you get a receipt showing that you have paid. If you go to another place and can't show the receipt, you have to pay again. There was a China man here that did not have the sense to show his receipt, and had to pay three times.

My job is to saw logs in the forest with a 7 foot saw alone. This is a monotonous life up here in the forest. You work 11 hours a day, eat three meals and the rest of the time you sleep. It is about the only way you can earn any money here in California. If it goes like I plan, (and it seldom does) I will stay here until I earn $300, and then buy some land in the fall.

June 9, 1912

Now I finally got a chance to write again. I was moved to another sawmill up almost twice as high in the mountain. I and a Norwegian rode up with Petterson, but we had to walk most of the way. Along the way we passed Big Creek, a waterfall that comes down from a 3000-foot-high hill. They are going to erect an electric power station and build a big dam so that they will have water all year round. The sawmill is 6800 feet above the sea level and lies in a dell. In three years' time, the water will be 100 feet deep. It is San Joaquin Light and Power that is doing the work. They employ about 3000 workers. Most of them are "Dagos"--southern Europeans.

When we finally got up to the mill, I was soaked with sweat, tired and hungry. It was snow and cold up there, so we went into a Norwegian's cabin and warmed up. Then we had to wait until 6 o'clock before we got any food. The worst of all is that we did not have a cabin, and had to sleep in an attic with the roof so low that if you sat up right, you got a bump on the head. We stayed there a week. I was so dissatisfied that I was tempted to quit.

Sunday, we started to build a cabin, myself and a man from Stockholm who forgot how to talk his mother tongue after living in the giant forest of California for 25 years. It was not done because the boss came and wanted us to work. They do not have any strict respect for religion here, so I worked until 5 o'clock. I later washed my clothes and now I think I will write and tell what happened.

Gust the man from Stockholm, is still doing carpenter work on our cabin. He just got his knapsack from Shaver where he worked before. The boss at Shaver was of the mentality that after a man had been there for two years it was time to fire him, so Gust got fired.

It is once in a while I get a longing feeling for the forests and valleys of my homeland, but I do not regret the desire to come here, but I long and wait for the time that I can travel back home. If all goes as I plan, then I will travel home for Christmas 1915.

It is nice to work together with Americans, and I now have one as my partner. It is unbelievable how fast the summer comes here, when we came up to two weeks ago there was 3 feet of snow, and now it is full summer. The grass is green (what there is of it) and warm during the day, but the wind is cold at night.

This is the third summer I have been with the forest, but never as high up in the mountains as we are now. I think I have written enough for this time, so now I am going to read instead.

June 13, 1912

Unlucky 13 has had its meaning for me today. I am so mad that this pen is shaking in my hand. Herman Petterson is a gentleman and since he does not have time to be here himself, he has a boss here. The boss is an old Irish man, and I have fallen out of favor with him. Sunday, he asked me if I wanted to work and I told him that I had to build a stove because it was cold in the cabin, then he said that I could do that next Sunday, so then I went to work. The other day I took a board home with me that I was going to use on the roof of the cabin, as luck would have it, when I got home, Thomas was standing by the cabin door. What are you going to do with that he asked? I'm going to use it on the roof, I answered in a disrespectful manner, since he has been giving me dirty looks. He told Gust at dinner, that when Herman comes, he was going to ask him if he could fire me. Since I have never been fired before, I did not want to be fired now, especially when you work for Herman Petterson. So I asked for my time. If it wasn't for his age, I would have shown that old Irish man what a pair of Swedish fists can be used for. Now I don't know how it will go with the $300. I'm going to Petterson's other mill in the morning and ask for work and if I don't get any then I will go to the oilfields, they pay good there, but is also very hot there too.

June 25 Petterson's Mill, Tollhouse, California

It is Tuesday night. I am tired and have a pain in my back. I rode with a Teamster here from the other mill and got a job right away. It is a job for two men and I am paid $65 a month, that's why I am so tired. It is very hard on my back, so I don't know if I want to stay here. If I stay three or four months it will bring me closer to the $300 I need.

July 10, 1912

It is Wednesday night and I am tired as usual, such hard work and such poor pay I haven't had since I was here before. It is so warm during the day that I am soaked with sweat all the time. We have good water up here, and that we use. It is melted snow that comes down from the mountains and in the afternoon, it is warm enough to bathe in.

August 3, 1912

It is almost never that I write in my book, but I don't have much to write about. "Everything goes its happy way". In July, a Swedish boy quit here. He was promised $55 a month, but when he quit the bookkeeper would not give him more than $45. He said that a young fellow like him wasn't worth more. The boy that fired the steam engine before got $65 a month. It was then that we had to show the Danish bookkeeper, Pete Hansen, that he should be fair, when he had worthy Swedish workers. We told Axel that he should try once more. He did, but with the same results, then we all went into the office and told Pete that if he doesn't give Axel his money, then we would have to teach him. Not one man will do any more work until you give Axel his $55 a month. Later we sent Axel in again, and this time the damned Dane paid him, and that's what you have to do when they don't keep their promises. It is much cooler up here now, and I don't get as tired as I did at first. The boys are working half a day this Sunday, so I am going out and cook coffee for them.

September 25, 1912

I came to Fresno on Saturday, and now I am in Kingsburg with my cousin Thorston. I stayed in Fresno one night and it was so hot that I was soaking wet the whole night. We were up in the Zaps Park and bathed. They have bathing suits there, so men and women bathe together, *together*, understand.

I have earned $290 this summer, so it is gone somewhat as I planned. Now Bertil Swanson and I are going out to see some land that he bought down by the river.

Maybe I will buy land there too.

There is going to be an exhibition in Fresno next week and I think that I will go. I thought I would only stay here a few days, but when it gets hot, you get lazy and drowsy so I will stay at least a week. For the present time, I have vigor and $200 in the bank. I bought new clothes, a pocket watch, and a bicycle so now there is nothing more I want. Sometimes I think it is dumb to sit here and write like this, but then it can be nice to read later.

October 3, 1912

I am home alone today. Thorston and Ada are in Fresno at the exhibition and I am going on Saturday. I was there Monday night with Elfie, so she could get a place. In the morning, I am going to Carther's and on my bicycle to see what it is like there. On Monday, I am steering my course to Bakersfield and maybe work there in the oil fields.

I don't know how it will go with buying the land. One tells me to buy, and the other tells me not to. Thorsten wants me to wait until after the election. He says that if we get a Socialist or a Democrat we will have hard times, (Wilson – – Democrat 1913 to 1921) so I hope he wins.

California is the fly's promised land, that is for sure. It is full of them here and they look just like the ones in Sweden. I wish that I could see all of America at one time so that I could find the best place to live, and also be able to see three years into the future to know the best way to earn money.

It is like I have come to a Y in the road and don't know which way to go. Here are the ways:

1. Buy 20 acres of land by the river or 10 acres in Carruthers.
2. Get a job with a painting contractor.
3. Be self-employed.
4. Go to Coalinga.
5. Work in the marsh where they are going to drain out the water.
6. Loan out my money at 7%.
7. Put the money in land and maybe gain 30 or 40% or lose the little I have, $800 Swedish Crowns, and that can be soon gone if I speculate. What should I do?

October 14, 1912 Fresno California

It has been a week since I last wrote and I am still in the same situation. I and another boy went down to Bakersfield last week, but there was no work. We were out there where they pump up the oil. There are at least 2000 pumps and each one has its own steam engine and pumps up the oil like water. The oil is black and is used for heating and to oil the roads. It costs $.50 to go there and back again. When the oil is pumped up it is so full of sand and as thick as porridge. It then runs down into small dams were the sand sinks to the bottom and then the oil is clean.

We went back to Kingsburg and on Saturday I went to Fresno and got a job nailing boxes together for $.30 an hour. I paid a dollar for a place and went back to Kingsburg for my work clothes and Eric went with. When we got there, we could not take the job because we had never nailed boxes together before. We went back to Fresno and rented a nice room for one dollar a day. If I keep on like I am now, I soon won't have any money to worry about. I think that I will go and get a job in a winery. There you get $1.50 a day and food. That's nine dollars a week, but it is a nasty job.

October 24, 1912

I am back by Thorston again. Knut and I have bought land today. We bought 20 acres for $4020.

October 30, 1912

I have plenty of work now with painting. I earn $2.50 a day, get lunch and afternoon coffee. I have much more to do now than when I worked for the other painter. Thorston's wife and two boys are here for a visit. They are on a trip from their home in Nebraska to Washington and from there to here. They will stay a week and then go back home. They were born here and speak very good Swedish. They are so nice and pleasant that you can't help but like them.

January 2, 1913

Now once more a year is gone. Time goes fast in America. Maybe it's just because you eat three meals a day or because one day is just like the other so that you do not notice that you are moving forward in time.

When I am down here, I seldom think of Sweden, but at Christmas time my thoughts fly over the ocean to my home in the North. Christmas Eve we were by Lindholm's, and Christmas day we were by Guldbrands. The day after Christmas it was back to normal again. Knut and I thought so much about Sweden that we went down to our land and pruned some trees to help us forget. A person becomes so drowsy and dissatisfied that you don't care about anything. Each time I think I should write in my book, I put it off. It can wait.

We have now lived in the same place as last year, a month now, but will soon move.
Knut moved to a farmer today, and on Monday Arthur is moving to another. Later I too will move together with another boy. We were in town today and paid $300 on our land and on the 15th we will have to make another payment.

January 5, 1913

Tuesday night 8:30, I feel good in my body, not in spirit. I feel so sick that I can hardly sit still. That tortures me. I don't want to write down here – – maybe I will laugh about it in the future. To be sick in spirit is worse than being sick in your body.

Today has been so cold that I think I froze more in California than I did in Sweden. It has not been more than 34 Fahrenheit and in this climate, you feel the cold more than you do in a cold climate. In the morning, I am going to start a job that should last a month. Right now, I am painting a buggy. I got a letter from Sweden that I should answer, but I don't feel like writing now. The way I feel now, I don't care about anything.

February 24, 1913

It is Monday afternoon and I'm almost finished with that "big job" that I thought would last a month. It was six weeks instead. Now I don't have a job on hand, and if I don't get one, I will go and work on our land. There is plenty of work, but you don't get paid for it.

March 4, 1913

The rain is over and we have fine weather again. We went to a theater to see what a theater was like. To my shame I must admit that I had never been to a real theater before, so for me it was doubly pleasant for us to see the world's most skillful action actress, Mme. Sarah Bernhardt from Paris. She appeared in the French play "UNE NUIT DE NOEL"--"ONE CHRISTMAS NIGHT". Mme. Bernhardt is 68 years old, but she looked like she wasn't more than 25 or 30 when we saw her, and she moved as easily as a 20-year-old.

I have just read the Swedish American and now I am preparing lunch, then I am going out to the farm and see if I can burn up some branches. I read in the paper today that Woodrow Wilson is taking over the office of President of the United States.

April's 27th 1913 Shaver Camp 11

I am sitting here with my knapsack on my knee and writing. It is Sunday afternoon. I haven't written in my book for a while because there was nothing to write about, but now I have something to write, so it won't hurt to have it written down.

We went up in the forest this year the same as before, but did not get work in Petterson's Mill, so we went higher up to a big mill that is called Shaver. It is the biggest mill on this mountain and like the other sawmills, the men are treated like dogs. All the bosses are Irish and the cooks are Chinese and the food is more fitting for swine than for humans. Last year I got $65 a month and good food, but this year I will only get $40 a month if that much. Such food and rough workers as here, you would never dream of seeing in our cherished Motherland.

I bought a camera in Kingsburg and have taken a dozen shots. When I get them I think I will paste them in this book.

Crew at Shaver's

The time goes slow up here. You just eat and watch the clock, and each time you think it should be later. We are six that are from Smaland and one from Vastergotland that is about 32 years old. He is the worst person I have seen that can amuse people. When you just look at him, you have to laugh. He was born in Goteborg and has been out in the world since he was six or seven. If you can believe what he says, he has been all over the world.

"Knallen" and two of us have been working this Sunday, and as soon as the Vostergotlander will come in, as the work for the day is done. He is the buffoon here dressed in a pair of white plasterer's pants. If I get a chance, I'm going to take a picture of him.

Carl and Albrekt

April 29, 1913

Carl and I were up by a small tray-mill that they use when they pick fruit today and asked for work. They said that they are not going to start work for another two weeks, but we did not want to wait that long. We have been here four days and only worked two days so it is no use to say where we will go, for we have no demands on us. We are thinking of going down to big Creek in the morning and see if we can get work. It might be better than here. If we can get work down there, then I think I will stay a week or two, and then go down to Los Angeles and get a job with a painter. The worst of it is that, I am forced to earn money so that we can make payments on our farm. If we do not pay, I may have to leave everything. That would not be very pleasant after I have invested both time and money. Man must live on hope. Maybe things will get brighter. However it will be, I won't stay here. It is full of Irishmen and they generally have no manners. Some of them sit at the table with their hats on. I think that this outline can be used as a remedy for America fever. If I come home to Sweden and become dissatisfied there, then these pages in my book should cure me.

Carl

May 2, 1913

We went on the train to Shaver on Wednesday and when we got there, we took our knapsacks and blankets and headed for Big Creek. After we got about 3 miles, we met a man that was coming from there. He took a job in Fresno, and got a free ticket up there, but when he got there and saw what kind of work it was, he did not want to start. He was going to Shaver. He said that you could not get work in Camp Two unless you go down to Fresno and get a free ticket up and work four days to pay for that ticket. When we heard that, we turned around and went to Shaver and got our pay, which was $2.45 each. We sent our things to Cressman's, and with God, we happily started walking. When we came to the first crossroad, there was an automobile mechanic that broke down with his car. So we helped him take off some parts on his car. He was from Stockholm and came here as a child. His mother was Swedish and father American. He spoke Swedish to us, but talked English too fast. We each got $.50, so we were a little richer than before. We went from there to where Al lives (one of the boys) where we are now. We thought of going down to the Tollhouse at the same time, but then I thought that we could just as well stay a few days and later find some work. We have now worked one day and the night before. The Swedes we have met here have taken the job of cutting a path through the trees where they are going to run electric lines. They can earn six or seven dollars a day. They burn up the branches at night. When the job is done, they are going to Fresno and Kingsburg and have a good time.

When I was home in Sweden I heard that when a man put on a shirt in the USA he kept it on until it was worn out. I did not believe that until now. These boys have been here two months and in that time, they have not changed underwear, shaved or cut their hair. Their shirts are as stiff as pine bark around the collar and their other clothes are the same way. If you are going to earn money here that's the way you have to live. Carl is cooking beans for supper and I am writing in my book. We are three from Ostergotland, three from Smaland and two of us have tramped our baby shoes in Varmland, the beautiful and wonderful land – – – now Carl and I are thinking again of home, and there is no sense in thinking, but you do anyway.

The crew at Petterson's Mill

Albrekt

May 29, 1913

When I last wrote, I was in the wild forest. Now I am in the big town of San Francisco and living in a church, and have such a bad cold that I can hardly see. When I left the boys, a store keeper by the name of Cressman asked me if I would paint his garage, so I stayed a week and painted. Later they wanted me up in Petterson's Mill, so I went up there too. I didn't know how it was by Petterson's Mill this year, I didn't like it. I got $45 a month and had to work much harder than I did last year. It was a good place to stay with Cressman. The oldest daughter used to play and sing in the evening. She is not like other girls in general, here in America. She is not at all conceited (girls coming from Sweden are generally affected by that sickness). She looked like a farm girl in Sweden, but she is educated as a lady of the world. She can scrub the floor, play the piano, cook good food and take a camera in hand and go out on a fishing party. I sold my camera to Mrs. Cressman for the same price I paid for it.

Cressman's daughter

I went up to Camp 11 to see the boys, and then rode my bicycle 52 miles down to Fresno. I bought some new clothes and a new knapsack. I then went down to Kingsburg to visit my relatives, stayed a day, and then went directly to San Francisco and had a hard time to find the address I was looking for. Edman was not home so the priest took me in, and that evening I went to their prayer meeting and became acquainted with the painter. I got an address from one of them to a painting master. He was not home himself, but his wife said that he does not have work for any more men.

I was up in Golden Gate Park for a while and rode on a trolley down to Market Street. As I stood there, a young man came and talked to me. He said that he was an American and we talked about everything. As we talked a fellow came up to us and said that he wanted to talk to him. After a while they came back in the last fellow asked me if I knew the first fellow, or if I talked to him first. When I told him no, he then wanted to know what we had talked about and then he took out a police badge out of his pocket and said that he was a detective. Then he ordered the other fella to go with him, and by that way I had been saved from a con man. The detective recognized the con man's method of setting up a mark. It would not have been so easy to dupe me, as I had been burned before when I was in San Francisco. If I had never met one like that before, and had a couple hundred dollars in my pocket, and a detective never came, it is possible that under the influence of some narcotic I would've been drowsed off in some dark hole and been robbed of my money.

I live in a room upstairs in the church and am going to lay down a while and try to ease my cold. Right now, I don't have anything good to say about San Francisco. When I think about everything, I wish I had never left Sweden.

June 4, 1913 Oakland California

I must have too much of Cain's blood in my arteries. I never seem to stay in one place very long. I am now going to Big Creek. I got a job with the painter in Oakland on Sunday and got three dollars a day for eight hours. I was promised work for a couple of weeks. The worst of it was, that no matter how hard I worked, it was not enough, and the smell of turpentine was so strong in my head, that I felt like I was drunk all the time. Add to that the expense of living in a town--- one dollar a day for room and board, car fare, shaving, wash, and then be without work and pretty soon you cannot even support yourself.

I went to an employment office today and got a job. I get free transportation and we leave tonight. I wonder how soon I will get a job that I will be satisfied with. There is so much to see in San Francisco, but I don't think much of the small towns on the side of the bay.

Oakland

June 6, 1913   The Wild Forest

The last time I wrote in this book, I was in a hotel in Oakland, and now I'm sitting on my blankets with my knapsack on my knee for a table. We left San Francisco on Wednesday night we were in Fresno by 5 a.m. and then rode the company train up here. I met the boss on the train that the boys work for in the Spring. He wanted me to stay and work on his farm, while he went up to Alaska. The pay was $45 a month and food. The worst of it was that I would have to live alone and I did not like that idea very much, so it was "no pants with that coat". It is so full of mosquitoes here that I thought I was being eaten alive. Anyway, I went up to the camp and thought that if I could get a good job, I can just as well stay here as anywhere else.

When we got up there, we had to live in tents and sleep in an iron bed and got two blankets to lay on.

Food was not too bad. In the morning when I saw what kind of work I was to do, I decided to quit at noon.

We got a free train right up here, but were expected to work five days to pay it off, and so today in the morning, I took a lunch pail with me and left. Good, that I took the lunch pail and would not have to sleep hungry that night. I went along a round about way so as not to be noticed. After I had gone 7 or 8 miles through brush and over hills and even though I took a roundabout way, I met one of the bosses. He asked if I came in yesterday. I told him that I had been there a week. He said that it was mean of me to take the lunch pail, and that I could not deny. Yes, I cheated the big power company out of 4 1/2 days and lunch pail, and since I have no reproach, either my conscience was asleep or it was not such a serious offense.

I'm in a place about 8 miles from Pettersons and 2 miles from Cressman's and 1 mile from Armstrong. It is 6 miles to Ockeden and in the morning, I am going up there and telephone Nelson's Mill. If I don't get work there, I will go to Camp 11 in Shaver, and if I don't get work there, then I don't know how it will go. If I do get work, I will stay until fall. That I must do!

June 9 Camp 11 Shaver

I slept in the woods that night, and in the morning, I jogged along to Ockenden then, with my pack. I met a Teamster that wanted me to go with him to Nelson's Mill and get a job there. I went with and stayed half a day. In the morning, I went to see if the boys were still there. The same ones were there that came up in the Spring. I thought that I could just as well stay there, and then we would be half a dozen. There were no Swedes in Nelson's Mill and what was worst, was that there were no cabins, and so that night I had to sleep out in the shed. I am now in the place I first came to last spring, and now I must stay here until we all go down at one time. I am to start in the afternoon. I wonder what I will do?

June 13, 1913 Camp 11

I am not superstitious, but it looks like the number 13 has had an effect on me. For a year now, since I last wrote in my book, I have met unlucky 13. This year I won't get by that date either it seems. It has gone crazy for me the whole year, and now it is time that I got on the right track. I started work Tuesday morning and had a job to do various things. I had that job a day and a half, and then I got another job where they load logs. That is the most boring job I have had. I had to shovel dirt and branches and debris that was left when they dragged out the logs. The worst of it is was that when I had nothing to do, and still had to keep busy.

If the boss saw that I had nothing to do, he always had some hole to put me in to shovel. Today it was worse than before, so by noon my patience was at an end. When we went home to eat lunch, I stayed home. (If you can call such a place as this home). In the morning, I'm going to ask Adam if he has another job for me and if he doesn't----so goes one more time on life's highway. If he does have a job for me and I don't like it, I will quit and go someplace else. I would rather stay here. The food is better than last year but there's not much of it.

Either I have bad luck or am a man that is not

satisfied with anything, but one thing is certain, is that I have never been dissatisfied with the job because it was hard work. When a person has nothing to do and still pretend that you are working, it is like eating pancakes when you don't have any.

June 15, 1913 Sunday

I asked Adam if he had another job for me because there was nothing to do in the one I have, I said, and then he said, "what are you complaining for?" I will give you a job, so that you will have to work like the devil! Instead, I got a job that is so easy that I can sit and rest half the time, and now I am satisfied.

While we ate breakfast this morning I was thinking how it was in Sweden on Sunday morning. There they sat dressed in fine clothes and ate good food at a finely set table. Here they sit on long benches and slobber in the food like swine. Most of them have their hats on and amuse themselves by throwing biscuits at each other. Such is life up here and oddly enough it goes quite well.

June 19, 1913

It is Saturday morning and there are only three of us left. We were six yesterday. Carl did not like his job, so he left yesterday. Arthur and I told the timekeeper that we wanted our time.

He got mad and said to me, "you were up here in the Spring and quit!"

"Yes, I was, and now I'm going to quit again!"

"No, he said, you will never get a job here again!"

"That's okay because I don't want any here!"

He said, "you are no good after all!"

"Then I am just like you."

After this exchange of words, he got so mad that he ran up the stairs to the cookhouse and then to the branch office to save his rank, honor and dignity. Arthur and I then had a good laugh. We ALL quit. We were tired of getting abuse from the people in charge and now we are leaving. Maybe we will go to Big Creek. Anyway, we are going down to Shaver, and then later we will see what we will do.

June 30, 1913

I am sitting in a wooden box that we call a bed with my knapsack on my knee for a table writing with a pen I made myself out of a piece of wood.

Arthur and I went down to Shaver and there we met Carl. We thought that we would go to the East, but then thought we could just as well wait until noon. While we waited a man came and wanted workers to go to Nelson and Bretz Mill so we went. We have been here a week now. I am sawing logs in the forest. It is hard work, so hard that I don't think I will keep on with that.

I'm very homesick during the day. I sometimes think of going home next Christmas and I can save enough money for that, but then I think that it is better to wait until 1915 and then sell the land and go and stay home.

There are so many expenses on our land that I don't know if we can hold onto it. If we can, I figure that I will have 6-7000 crowns when we sell it in the fall of 1915, and then I will steer my course to Sweden. Yes, the air castles are over with.

Later I think I will set up a store with my brother Gunnar, get married and then stay home. I will have to learn a few things, but I'm not afraid of that.

When I am out here in the forest sawing logs, I just think of the time when I will again see mother Svea (Sweden), and my mother, and brothers and sisters. I have never regretted coming here, but I have never planned on staying here. I long for Smaland's smiling meadows and sighing forest and I wonder if I will ever get home again. The other boys here are more homesick than I.

July 13, 1913

It is Sunday, so now we can rest after the week's grind and toil. I saw logs in the forest all day. It is very hard work, so when I come home at night I go straight to bed. It is so hot in the sun, that after you work a while you are soaked with sweat, and on your back it becomes frothy where your suspenders are. If my future plans are fulfilled, I have earned them, after going through hell's fire, that is for sure!

When I don't have anything else to do on Sunday to pass the time, I can just as well write down what I have seen in San Francisco. You can't see much of a city in a few weeks, anyway I will write a little of what I did see. I have written before that San Francisco is a city worth seeing, and that is certain.

SAN FRANCISCO

The Golden Gate City Gate Park

The city has a population of 1 million people. It is built on the Bay of the Pacific Ocean on sandhills. There is hardly a flat place in the whole city. Market Street is the biggest street and so busy, that if you want to cross over to the other side you need eyes in the back of your head so that you can get across with all of your skin. The city is just as big as it was before the earthquake. It has raised itself up from the ashes like a miracle. The highest buildings are 15 to 20 stories high. That is nothing compared to New York's skyscrapers, but I think they are high enough. If you want to get away from the hustle and bustle of the city, you can take a trolley out to the beach or Golden Gate Park. I was at the park on Sunday. It is the biggest and finest park I have ever seen. It is 6 miles long and full of small dams and grottoes and flat lawns to sit and play on, here and there are posters of America's most thought of people.

There are all kinds of animals, beers, buffaloes, kangaroos, elks and deer in large cages.

There is a big band shell where they play music for three hours every Sunday. They also have a big museum filled with all kinds of interesting things. If you were to see everything in this museum it would take a whole day, and everything in Golden Gate Park can be seen for free. Out on the beach it is full of people sunbathing and watching the sky-high waves. If you follow the shoreline a little way you come to Cliff House. It is built on the shoreline way out over the cliff. There is much to see. For $.10 you can use a pair of binoculars and see the freighters and sailboats out in the ocean. You can see the seals laying in the sun, sunning themselves. It is best to be dressed warm because the wind is strong on the West Coast.

Now for the last, we will make a visit to Chinatown. The life there is very lively. I don't know if it is so dangerous now, but before the earthquake you could easily disappear if you went in alone. When you come to the beginning of Chinatown the police are there and offered to go with you on the streets. It was broad daylight so I went alone. It was like you came to a town in China. Houses are built in Chinese style and all the people were dressed like they are in China. Both men and women are dressed in pants. The shops sell all kinds of wares, both Chinese and American. Most of the shops sell masses of fish, lobster and crabs and naturally there are the town hookers. Nels Edman, the man I lived with in San Francisco is a strongly religious man. Even so, I got him to go with me one night to see the seedy side of the town. It couldn't hurt to see the misery, but you can't help but feel pity for the young pretty girls that spend their lives there. Some of them have come of their own free will and some of them have been kidnapped and once they have been there it is not easy to get away.

There are about 2000 girls. Some are in a small room, and you press on a button and a girl comes out and opens the door, then you go in and pay a dollar, see them, stay a few minutes and then leave, but I did not feel like giving them a dollar. When I saw the depraved insolence, and over-powdered faces, I could not help but feel pity for them. Then there are the dance halls where you go in and dance with the girls, and drink beer and consort with the girls. We were in a few of them. As soon as you come in, you have two of these cosmetic beauties on either side of you. I'm usually not at a loss for words, but that time I was. There were a few Swedish girls in the last dance hall we were in. They came and wanted us to buy them a beer. They had a first-class band, and you could either dance with a girl or sit and drink beer and watch. If you bought a girl a drink it cost $.50 and she got a ticket for $.40, but Edman and I were too big of fish to hook. When we were going to leave, a big fat Swede came and stood in Edman's way. Since he did not want to have an exchange of words with her, he put his big hands on her and then she moved aside. Then we went out to the street, and at the last of this little description, I should mention that in the middle of all of this activity the Salvation Army had a mission.

July 14, 1913

Once again, the knapsack is laced up and we are on our way. Erik and I are going to Kingsburg to pick fruit. I went home at 3 o'clock in the afternoon to pack my things and tonight after I get my check, I will go to Camp 11 and stay the night. Then we will walk the long 18 miles to Tollhouse in the morning.

July 30, 1913

I am now at the last page in this book, and next time I write I will start a new one. I am now in Kingsburg, living with one farmer and working for another. I get two dollars a day for 10 hours work. It is a good job. Sometimes it is hot, but that you don't pay much attention to. I have it good and in all ways, so now I don't think of Sweden so much. Once in a while we go swimming down by the river, that is very refreshing.

The best of all are the nights, they are so warm and delightful that you could not ask for better. If I had a horse and buggy I could invite a girl and go out riding, but without the aforementioned things you can't have it so nice out here in the country. I have never been down here during the summer before and this summer is not like the others. It does not rain, and no one here can remember when it did rain this time of the year. If I could earn just as much money down here as up there, I would never go back to the forest again.

I think that we will be forced to sell our land in the fall. We can hardly pay the expenses on it. The trees have grown so much this summer, so that I didn't recognize them when I went down there.

End of Book 2

(Note: This journey took 32 days)

BOOK 3

October 11, 1913, Kingsburg California

I am sitting in my newly set up darkroom writing in my book. It has been a long time since I last wrote and I don't know why I took it out now. I am living in the same house as last winter and have the same comrades as before. I have just finished painting my cousin's house, TH Nelson. The days are just the right temperature this fall, and no rain as yet.

November 4, 1913

We have just moved to another house. Knut, Sven and myself and two boys from Varmland. We moved here the 31st of October and plan on staying the whole winter.

We have plenty of work, but none that we get paid for. We worked on our land and dug up a bunch of Johnson grass. It is a grass that was brought here from the East by a man named Johnson, hence, the name. He thought that it would be good fodder, but instead it has become a very troublesome weed. We have worked at that for couple of weeks, and then got the canals in order, pruned the trees and the grapevines. November 1, we have to pay $175.00 interest on the land and on January 15 we have to lay out $85. We have no money and if we can't borrow any in Kingsburg or get a hold of some money soon, Eklund can take back the land and we will lose all the money we have already laid out.

The way it is now, is no laughing matter, but that we do so anyway. We don't think about how we stand, without good humor. We have engaged a land agent to sell our land for $5000 and I hope we get it sold so that we can get away from our troubles. It is unusually nice weather today, 65° warm. Today I have seen the snowcaps for the first time this fall.

November 21, 1913

We were down on our land yesterday and dug up Johnson grass. We are still hard up for money now, and if we can't come up with $175 for the interest, Eklund can take the land from us without any trouble. I have been to three banks trying to borrow money and have been turned down on each time.

Wednesday, I wrote a letter to a boy in Toluma County and asked if he could loan me the money---his answer was "farewell to the land and start over". If we leave the land now, I'll lose $500. With that much money, I could go home to Sweden.

November 22

A while ago, Knut went out to see if we had any mail. We are waiting for a letter from Oscar with some money. Tuesday is the last day for paying the taxes. I think they will be about $40. I am so anxious that I don't know what to do. If we don't get the money before the 1st, all hope is gone. We have $33 or $45 coming from the raisin company, but don't know how soon we will be paid. Maybe today. Knut just came home and there was no letter.

Carl and Knut

Rented House

Roommates

November 23, 1913

I got a letter from Oscar today, but no money, even though he could afford to help us if he wanted to. Here you experience the truth in the saying" a friend in need is a friend indeed". We are thinking of going to another bank in the morning and see if we can borrow the money for the taxes, and then go down to Visalia and pay them.

I am now going to try and give Oscar Petterson a fitting answer to the presumptuous letter I got yesterday. I wrote him so humbly, that I was almost ashamed, but it will be different this time, that is for sure.

November 28, 1913

We were at the bank today and were able to loan the money for Eklund so the next blow we will have to take will be January 15. So now we can feel secure for a little while. In the morning, we are going to work full force on our land and maybe be done before Christmas. We have especially nice weather these days. It rains almost every day and that is the nicest weather you can have in Fresno County this time of the year.

Albrekt Lundquist

January 1, 1914

Another year has sunk down in the ocean of time

and now we are in the beginning of a new year. I can wonder what that will bring.

Since I came here, each year has gone smoother for me than the year before. 1910 I had my journey paid for, 1911, I could not get anything together. 1912, I earned $300 in the summer and bought land in the fall. For me 1913 was not so different than 1911, so after that figuring, 1914 should be for me the same kind of year.

I had work painting three weeks before Christmas and earned $50. Christmas Eve we were at Gulbranson's and that was very pleasant until 4 o'clock when a drunken pig came in and ruined everything, so we left right away. New Year's Eve, we went to the Mission Church in Kingsburg. There were about 100 people, and at the stroke of 12, they dropped down on their knees in silent prayer, except 12, and among them I was one.

When we went home, we were 10 or 15 boys together with three girls. The girls ran from one side of the road to the other like intoxicated hands and the boys behaved just as dumb. When we got home we had some sour milk and bread and later screamed and hollered like the worst cannibals for a while, and then we went to bed.

Yes, such is life in Kingsburg. Think! What a New Year's celebration! I hope I don't have to celebrate more than one New Year in America, especially in Kingsburg. The churches here ruin everything, so the young here are more dead than alive.

Kingsburg is a town about the same size as my hometown of Malmback. There are about 2000 people in and around the town. Kingsburg has five

Swedish churches and two English ones and each one has its own pastor on $1000 a year salary. Also, there are a few associations that have not built their own churches, instead, they rent the local's. Four and five times a year they have a so-called "revivalist meeting" and send for preachers from New York, Chicago, Minneapolis and many other places.

That is the way the Swedes are in Kingsburg. They have tried to rent the house that we live in and kick us out because they think we live a good for nothing life and are on the road to sin, but our landlord is a so-called "church hater", so I think that we will be able to stay here as long as we want. That is the way things are now, January 1, 1914.

February 6, 1914

We now have sun and warm days. It has not rained for over a week, but showers are sure to come before the sun appears. We have just pruned the trees and burned the branches so now we just have the grapevines again.

By the way, one of my cousins is building a house now. At Christmas time, he asked me if I wanted to paint it, so a few days ago I was down by him and figured out how much it would cost, and it came to $144. At that price, it would be $2.50 a day. Another painter came and looked at the work and wanted to do it for $105, $39 less than I would do it for, who believed that I would work cheaper when it was for a relative.

I am now going to paint the house for $105. The other painter in Kingsburg has promised to help me so that I can get the paint cheaper, and then maybe I will make $2.50 anyway, or at least $2.00. If I have to, I would work for $.50 a day just so Jansen could not underbid me. I'm going to buy the paint from the boss I worked for in Los Palos and then start to paint.

March 5, 1914

I am almost finished with the outside of Lindholm's house but do not have much to do now, because the carpenters are not done.

Lindholm's House

I listened to a social speaker the other night. He was a doctor of medicine. Among other things, he said that there are about 5 million people in the United States that have no work, no home, and when night comes, they don't know where they will sleep.

San Francisco alone has 20,000 people out of work and there are 120,000 women in the United States in prostitution. 18,000 young girls are kidnapped each year and most, when they go from one city to the other, and just about as many die through direct or indirect suicide.

There is a nightly "revival" for the residents in Kingsburg. There is a preacher here, an Irishman by the name of Dan Shannon. He is here to scoop up "Life's Waters" in the amount of $2-3000, or however much it will be. He took in $3000 in Selma when he was there. He has been here a month and will be here another week.

I have heard him several nights. (He has a meeting in a big tent every day and three times on Sunday). He strikes me as a person better suited as a comic rather than a preacher. Everything that does not strike his fancy, he considers reasonable in the beginning, and if he senses that he has support, then he changes and reasons that it is impudent. They take up a collection each night before they start and before that you go out. They pass the collection plate again as he tells them that they should dig up $.50 or $.25, because he does not want to see any nickels.

Dan Shannon is a very gifted speaker. When he speaks you can't help but listen, and most of what he says is fact. The other night he had a meeting for freethinkers. He actually convinced them that God does exist. Among other things he said that, some don't believe that God exists, because they have not seen him. Man cannot see God, but can feel his power, man can't see the wind, but can feel its power, man cannot see love, but man can feel the power of love.

To start with, each night he cracks some jokes and says something witty to get the people in a good laughing mood, and when he says something especially good, they clap their hands as if they were in a theater. Then last, just before he stops preaching, he talks so touchingly and becomes thick in his voice and almost Christ. One can divide his preaching into three parts, first laughter, second seriousness, and third emotion. One night they converted 32 people and another between 40 or 50. All they had to do was go up and shake Dan

Shannon's hand and sit down on the first benches and have their names written down in the book and are then saved and have a cheerful disposition and are happy just to think of the future. "SIC TRANSIT GLORIA MUNDI" (Worldly Things Are Fleeting).

April 14, 1914

We have just finished watering our land, the vineyard and orchard. When we were down there, I saw a big spider, that I took home. It is very poisonous, enough to kill a man. I plan on keeping it and taking it home with me to Sweden. I would like to find a scorpion and a rattle from a rattlesnake to keep it company. To kill it, I tried to drown it. I put it in a glass jar, filled it with water and screwed the cap on tight, turned the jar upside down several times to make sure it was airtight. I then laid down for an hour before I checked at the see if it was dead, and to my big surprise it was just as lively as when I put it into the jar. Today I put it back into the same jar and filled it with alcohol and still the monster lived about 20 minutes in an airtight jar filled with alcohol. Now it is dead.

I have finished painting Lindholm's house. I earned $1.50 a day, thanks to Jansen for putting his nose into other people's business.

Sunday, April 18, 1914

It is very warm today, 91°, so now a person does not have to freeze. The boys are sitting out on the porch playing two card games. For my part, I have no interest in playing cards. I'm going to set the coffee pot out in the sand with the sun shining it's brightest so that I can have a cup of hot coffee this afternoon.

May 11, 1914 Camp 3   Hume

We are now up in the woods again. This is the fifth summer I am here and I hope it is the last, but that I have hoped every fall and have been disappointed every year. There has been a shortage of work everywhere we have been before. We could not go to Herman Petterson because he is not going to do any work this summer. My comrades and I are in Camp 3, the others are in Camp 4. The food here is somewhat good, but nothing to brag about. Tomorrow we are going to start sawing logs

It is Saturday night and 55° warm, we have put in five days up here now, and I wish that we were done and could go back down any day. We are sawing logs in the woods. Each man saws with a 6 or 7 foot long saw. It is very hard work, in particular, this week. At times, I've been so tired that I could hardly walk, but surprisingly I don't feel so tired tonight. Knut took a picture of me today that I have developed. It can be nice to have as a souvenir (I hope) of my last summer up in the woods. If we stay here this summer, we hope to earn enough money to hold us until the beginning of fall and next fall have our land sold, and then I will go to Sweden.

May 22, 1914

Now we have worked here 10 days, and it is going good. The work is not so hard now that we are getting used to it, and the food is good. The people here are quiet and decent that I was surprised, but there is one thing that I have never seen before or had trouble with, and that is--- wall lice. I built a bed Sunday and when it was finished, I laid down to read and thought that I would have it nice for a while, but all of a sudden, I felt something crawling on my neck and when I looked, the whole bed was full of wall lice as big as my little fingernail.

The other night I felt a bite on my neck and when I felt to see what it was, it was one of them. (One just dropped on the table) it was a brown, flat thing, full of blood. That is going too far when my Swedish blood is going to be used as food for American wall lice.

When I came in tonight the temperature was 50°, but thanks to a good fire, it is now up to 60°.

May 25, 1914

I don't have as much trouble now with those bloodsuckers we call wall lice. I built myself another bed yesterday Sunday. We went home in the afternoon at 3 o'clock. It rained the whole day and we were soaking wet. We ate supper outside and it rained the whole time. The boards we sat on were so wet that it just ran off of them, and the table was soaked. The temperature was 40°, so from that description one can get an idea of what it is like to be in the woods.

It has been raining several days now. When you

come up on the mountain you can see the clouds both over and under you and then all of a sudden, you are in the middle of one. It is exactly like being in a dense fog. In a while the cloud passes by and then the sun shines. The cloud that paid us a visit this afternoon decided to stay and keep us under a tight drizzle cold as ice, so we had to go home. I am now sitting here thriving well. I have just put a couple clumps of tar in the stove and it is 68° warm in here.

May 31, 1914

I had not thought of writing, but I just had an experience that I had not seen before and thought it would be worth writing down. As I laid on my bed reading the Swedish American newspaper, I felt a mild hardly noticeable sticking in my little finger. When I looked at it, there was a wall louse, golden color and as thin as paper. I got up and stood by the lamp to study it. I could not feel anything, but saw that the louse got redder and redder and swelled up like a water bag when you filled up with water. When it sat there for about a minute, I scraped it off with a knife. It then tried to run away and I quickly killed it on a newspaper, about a quarter centimeter of the paper was smeared in blood.

Tonight, I have a gnawing toothache and I am not interested in anything, not even bloodsuckers!

June 17, 1914

Much has happened since I last wrote. The second cook and one of the waiters got into a fight. The cook got fired and the waiter had a black eye for a couple of weeks. Some guys quit and some got fired.

My comrade quit the week before.

Now to the last happening, which happened tonight. There is a young machinist here, Swedish by birth and born in America. His fiancée was up in the woods watching them load big logs onto a railcar. Bill was going to cross over the tracks and talk to her. He walked on unused tracks next to a railcar that was being loaded with logs. The mishap happened at that moment, when a steel cable pulled down a log from the top of the car and chopped up his left foot above the ankle.

The first that I heard of the accident was the signal from the steam engine. That means that someone is injured. If it is eight blasts it means that it is near fatal or fatal, which is worse is hard to say: **dead or crippled for life**. The whole thing was sad. The thought crossed my mind what if that had been me?

Sunday, June 21, 1914

I have rested all day today and now I am so tired and drowsy, as if I had done hard labor instead. When you rest and are not tired, then you become tired. I get $2.69 a day. I have to pay $20 a month for the food and one dollar for the doctor, so I have about $50 a month left. The tax collector was here Wednesday and got his tributes of $4.00. I could've done the same as some of the others have done, look him in the face and say that I have paid and have the receipt in my cabin. It could happen that he would believe me and cross out my name, but it is right to pay the taxes, and besides, I don't want to be a liar for $4.00.

Because of the poor times, we are not going to fell anymore timber now, instead we are going to saw up all that is been cut down and then I think we will all be laid off. I am sawing together with two Swedes that cut down trees before. We are about as lazy as we can be, and the lazier we are, the longer the work will last.

June 27, 1914, Saturday night

They have been around with a list this week to collect money for Bill Johnson, the one that lost his left foot. Here, the company does not have to pay anything, like they do in Sweden. I gave $1.00 and one worker gave $25. Jones, the super-intendent gave $40 but he can afford that more than I can afford $1.00. There is going to be a lottery July 4 for a car, $1.00 ticket, and 350 tickets. If the lucky winner wants to sell the car back, he will get $100 for it so there will be $250 left over, a scam to make money! If for example, I were to win it, I would rather sell it to anyone for $50, then sell it to the present owner $400. It is quite warm now during the day.

July 5, 1914

Today is the day after America's big celebration. It has been 90° all day in the shade and in the sun over 120°, but how much I don't know, because my thermometer does not go any higher. Yesterday we went to Finger Rock and I took some photos there. A German was there with a camera and took six pictures that I developed, and tonight I'm going to print them on paper. Maybe some of them will have the honor of being in this book.

July 9 Camp 6

We are up in the redwoods. I am dissatisfied with everything, except the climate and the stately trees. I have made photos for over $10 since Sunday. I forgot my money, writing, and most of the things I had in Camp 3 today. If I don't like it here better in the future, I'm going to quit and go back to Kingsburg.

Albrekt

Albrekt

July 10

Today I worked together with the Greek, and that was all. Tonight I quit. I burnt branches! This day has been as long as a whole week. Maybe it was dumb to quit, but now it is done.

"The Greek"

July 19, 1914, Kingsburg California

I came down Monday night and slept in a hammock the first night. I have been down on the land and watered every day since I came back down here, and now it is done. My companion and cousin Knut has given up his part of the farm and enlisted. (In the Army). He left our Fatherland to avoid military service and then enlisted in a foreign country for four years!

There are four other boys who have done the same thing. Now, Knut's siblings have his part of the land, so now there are four in the company. They want me to either get another companion, or they want to buy my part too.

My bicycle is broken, so I can't ride, and if I go into town to get it repaired I have to pay for it and then I will have to cash the check I got in the woods. If I take it to the bank, they will wonder why I don't pay something on the loan I have there, so now I have a hard dilemma to get out of. I have done 4 or 5 dozen photo postcards that I'm going to send up to the woods tomorrow morning, but the worst is that I have already gotten the money for them and that too is gone. It is very warm and the flies are absolutely crazy. I'm going to start sleeping outside now.

July 21, 1914

Saturday afternoon 5:30. The temperature is 98°. It is much warmer at noontime. I have not had much to do for a few days, but next week there will be much to do, and everything will be in a hurry. I have been picking peaches for a few weeks. It is not very hard work, but it is hot as a frying pan and you feel like a strip of bacon on a red-hot pan. The sand gets so hot that you cannot kneel on it, it also burns right through the soles of your shoes. I hope I don't have to stay here much longer. The climate here is more suitable for an African than it is for a Scandinavian. I took some photos of the trees and the fruit, but when I developed them and hung them up to dry, moths came and crawled on them so now they are ruined.

August 17

Now it is night and nice and cool 85° but the day was hot. It was warmer than usual, about 110°. I have taken new photos and have put a net over them so that the moths can't get on them.

Some people have overheated this week. There is a young Swede that was overheated the other day and is still senseless. A Mexican was also overheated. He was standing and crying when the farmer saw him, but he is all right now. Yes, here it is too hot, a person cannot feel well.

September 14, 1914

It is night, cool and nice now and the days are not too hot now. The days are 90 and 95°, so now it is fine.

Now to write something about the day's big question "the war"? Can a person think of anything more unnatural and useless than a war? People go out and kill each other on someone else's orders. Many are lucky enough to be without being crippled for life. The ones that are responsible sit home and feel good and stir up disagreement and hate to make it easier to get them to mutilate and murder each other. Such things can happen in the world's civilized countries.

The most Swedes here in America side with Germany and Austria, mostly because Germany is against Russia. Some scream and shout that Sweden should reunite with Germany and take Finland back, but they are generally people that do not have any close relatives to send out to the war. If one is to be just, you can hardly hold with Germany in this war, because Germany was clearly the aggressor in this war and assault by force it was. Belgium was neutral, but Belgium was just a breakfast bite for Germany, but they thought otherwise.

Sweden is neutral, and I hope it stays that way. Germany has repeatedly urged Sweden to declare war with Russia and take Finland again, but I hope the government in Sweden is intelligent enough to stay calm until you're forced to defend themselves. If it should come to that point, I am not against going home to defend my dear Fatherland, but I am not in favor of going home if Sweden should declare war.

I both believe and hope that this war will not last long. Germany and Austria have so many against them that they will soon be forced to give up. I do not believe that they will take Paris.

Everything is more expensive in Sweden now than before and the "war prices" have reached far-off California. All foodstuffs have gone up in price, on some things they have doubled, so in some ways we all suffer from the war as well.

September 28

For four or five weeks I saw an ad in the paper about a wash machine that costs $1.50, weighs 3 pounds and washes a tub of clothes in 3 to 6 minutes. I sent for one and now have it here. It is surprisingly good. I don't believe that my shirts have ever been as clean as they are right now. I have been invited to be the only agent in Fresno County and if no one else is ahead of me, I will be the agent and earn good money.

October 2, 1914

Fresno County Fair started this year on the 29th of September, and will close on the 4th of October. Yesterday was Kingsburg Day. Southern Pacific Railway had a pleasure trip and charged $.65 to go back and forth. There were all sorts of paintings as usual. There were even some flying machines, but they were all damaged, so those we did not get to see fly. There was an air balloon that they sent 1200 feet high up in the air. The gondola had room for five passengers. The ticket for this ascension to heaven cost $1. I then thought that if you can get up to heaven for a $1.00, I might just as well go up there for a while. I then bought a ticket and hopped into the gondola. The balloon went straight up at a dizzying rate of speed until we came to 1200 feet, the length of the line, that was to pull us back down to earth again. When we were up there, we could see the whole of the San Joaquin Valley, with all its vineyards, orchards, towns and rivers, so it was well worth a dollar after all.

Now this book is full, so I will start on another.

END OF BOOK 3

BOOK 4

Kingsburg California October 12, 1914

Now I am going to start a career as an itinerant peddler, businessman, or whatever I should call myself. Yesterday I got two letters and today I got two more from the company. Up to now, I have not gotten any more machines. I have four dozen on the way, but it is a long time before I get them because the distance from here to Ohio is quite long. I think I will get the first one on Wednesday and by the end of the week I should have the first dozen. In a few weeks three dozen more should come, and if I can sell them I should be able to sell more. If I did not have the farm, I would send for 12 dozen at the same time, but I don't have the money. All the money that I have goes to pay off on the farm.

October 13

Now I have gotten a pen that I can write like a man with, but my style is so uneven and pointed that no matter what kind of pen I have, it is not good anyway. Maybe the fault is that my fingers are too short or because of too little effort. I should write well now, if I am to be an agent and write to the company firm occasionally. I sold the first machine today and earned $.43 on the sale, but when I get going and manage to sell a few gross, I will earn a dollar a piece on them, if I get that far.

October 14

I have just gotten up and had coffee and now I don't have anything to do in my loneliness other than to sit here until 10 o'clock when the mail comes. I think I will get a machine today, but that is not certain. It is very boring to live alone like this, no one to talk to, and nothing to do.

October 17

Saturday night, 10 minutes before 10, I have just come home from Kingsburg. I get the first dozen wash machines Thursday and now today and yesterday I have been out demonstrating. I sold three and left out eight on trial. There is no dancing or frolicking when I come to the farmers. I have felt something between a criminal and a evildoer – – – in some places, doing such a favor. I left machines on trial and in some places, I could not. They saw the machines as something so bad that they did not want to soil their hands on it. I have scared horses and mules off the road when I came with the machines on my bicycle, but I am a genuine Smalander so it is not easy to discourage me. It is always a little lean in the beginning if you try something new. I will use "the ant and the grasshopper" as an example and want to be just as determined as the ant.

October 20

I was back to two places today where I left machines on trial. At the first place, they had not tried the machine, but are going to keep it anyway. I am going to get a load of wood as payment for it. At the other place, I had to take the machine back because they said it was useless, and now I don't have the heart to go to the other place. It is not pleasant to have to take back an article that has been left on trial. This afternoon I am going to a couple more places, but first I have to strengthen myself with a good dinner so that I won't faint when I have to take my wash machines back. The machines are good and only cost $1.50 and anyway, I have to take them back. Makes me wonder if all of them know how to use them. If I get too many back, I won't take any more, but those that I bought I will have to take.

October 31

I now have my eyes open concerning the wash machines and have come to the conclusion that I am no good as a salesman!!! What I saw as a genuine pearl has changed into a soap bubble that has already broken. Out of the first dozen machines, by grace, I sold eight and got three back. One of them is still out and I don't know if they will keep it or not and I am not going there to find out. They can have the machine just as well as me.

I rented a horse and buggy yesterday to go out and sell wash machines. By grace, I sold five, and in order to sell them, I had to lower the price. I sold two for $1.25 and three for $1.00 apiece. I earned $2.25 on the machines and paid $2.00 for renting the horse and buggy. I then had $.25 left for going out to the houses and feeling like a beggar or something of that sort. Yes, that is how it is to be a salesman. It is more like a path of thorns than a rose garden. Yesterday I sold a machine for four bottles of beer that I treated the boys on.

November 5, 1914

Two days have gone by since the big election day in America. The most burning question is to have prohibition or not. Some counties have prohibition, and Fresno County is one of them. Those that want intoxicating drinks go under the name of "wet" and those that want prohibition go under the name of "dry". Here there has been a mighty battle before the election. If the vote is "dry", it will be for eight years, and if it is "wet" it will be eight years more before they can do away with the booze again.

November 15, 1914

North Coast Mill   Fort Ross, California

It was about two votes "wet" against one vote "dry", so for now, they will have their saloons in the state.

Since I became tired of selling wash machines, there was nothing else to do but to go out on some sort of work. I am now at a sawmill and have Herman Petterson for a boss. This place is about 60 miles north of San Francisco right on the ocean shore. Myself and another boy traveled up here together. I threw my knapsack in the wagon and off we went over so many hills that I almost thought that we had encountered someone like the person I rode with in an automobile in 1911.

The driver told us that when we got close to the

ocean that we could get a room for $.50 each. When we came up to the hotel, they wanted $1.00 for each man. I then told them that I never paid more than $.50 in San Francisco, and then they gave us a room for $.50.

At last we got to Petterson's Mill and got a promise of work, but we would have to wait until the mill started up. In the meantime, I did duty as a night watchman in the sawmill. That is work that does not appeal to me, to go there alone and put on a great show. You don't have to work, but the time goes awfully slow when you don't have anything to do. I was sleepy the whole night, and not permitted to sleep and today when I can sleep, I am not sleepy. I don't feel good now and I have to go on watch duty again tonight

The cook personnel here are from far off China, so one can imagine how good the food will be.

We have now sold the land for $5700. That will be after the debts are paid. My part is $600.

If I get this money I can go home to Sweden, the time I had planned on. If I stay here until I have $400, then I will have enough money to go home on... I am not persevering, otherwise I would have more than I do. I have always chosen to be in places where I can live like a man, but there you cannot earn any money. In order to make money here, you have to live like an animal. There are many that have become rich in this country, but not by working, rather by speculating. Yes, such is life! One thing is certain, I would rather work hard during the day than be a night watchman.

November 18

I have now spent four nights out in the mill. It is going good at night. Most of the time I sleep, but during the day when I can sleep, I can't. The timekeeper came around today and asked me what time I sleep. I said I sleep when I get sleepy and am lying here waiting to fall asleep.

At night when I go out to the mill, I sit and read until 9 o'clock. Later I spread some skinny sacks on a 2-foot-wide wall that surrounds the boiler, and there I sleep until 4 o'clock. That is the time to get up and start a fire under the boiler. It is not a very good bed, but it is the best place, because if you get too far away from the boiler, I freeze. I have to lay very still, if I roll down from this 6-foot wall, I can easily break my neck off.

It is sunny and warm during the day and green grass is on the ground all over. November is the finest month of the year here on the coast. It is somewhat mischievous to be a night watchman at night you are alone, and the same during the day. At night, all the others are sleeping, during the day they are at work and during the day I have to be careful not to show myself, otherwise the authorities will get on me for sleeping during my working hours.

November 29, 1914

It is Sunday and the time is 4:30. I am sitting in the four corners box (that we call a bed) with my knapsack at my side as a table. The air is clean and clear. Here and there a few light clouds float by. The temperature is 45° and I am almost freezing. The sun goes down a little before 5 o'clock. It has rained a few days and more is coming. Myself and two other boys live in an old shed. There is no stove and no windows and it is very damp, the roof leaks and rains on us at night.

We now have a new cook, an American woman, and the food is almost worse than when the Chinese prepared it. IT IS BAD!!!

I have been a night watchman for 10 nights now and may continue for some time. I have three "donkeys" to fire up each morning, and this morning, the saw will be fired up, and I think I will have plenty to do with that. The "donkeys" will have to wait, but it could happen that the night watchman will have to "take his bed and go" if he does not do as he has been ordered.

November 30, 1914

It is so windy and cold today that in order to survive you have to stay in by the stove and tonight I have to be out in the mill. I have fired up three donkeys and three boilers. That is taking advantage of me, but if I don't do it, it could happen that I will get fired. I don't want to quit at this time. Last night I lay down and slept until 4:30 so when you watch like that, it is not very hard work.

December 2

Something happened yesterday that I have never seen in my whole life. I was on watch the last night between the 30th and December. 1 There was a terrible storm. The rain came down from the East and the wind was terrible. In the morning, the moon shone over the ocean between broken skies and mirrored itself in the Pacific Ocean and at the same time created one of the most beautiful rainbows on the rain clouds. That was the first strange thing that happened. The other came in the form of a communiqué from the high authorities that all work is to stop because the company does not have any money, so we don't know when we will be paid. Herman Petterson went to San Francisco today. He is going to get enough money so that each and every one can get down to Fresno. It has rained here for a day, but now there is a little pause. We have to wait here until Petterson comes back, and that can take as long as a week. When he finally does get back he may not have any money with him area all this depends on one of the company's members in San Francisco that is a swindler. There are many that have bought shares in the company and gave money to him. He then put the money in his own pocket. Now, just because of the trouble he has caused, 60 people are out of work. Most of them have traveled long distances to get here at great expense and now it could happen that they will lose that money plus their wages. Probably by law, we will be able to take out our money if there is anything to take.

December 6, 1914

Now we got part of our money. I got all of mine. The ones that had over $20, got only $20 and a note for the rest. Only the birds know if they will ever get any money on their notes. Herman Petterson had been to Fresno and got some money. I have only $14, but anyway, I'm glad to leave this place. It rained on us every night in bed, the food we got cannot be called food and we don't get any coffee, it is just un-adulterated chicory. Maybe we can leave in the morning, and maybe we can't go now. The road is slippery from all the rain, so you can hardly drive on it.

December 10, 1914 San Francisco

I am sitting in my room on Howard Street writing. We got here the night before last. It was raining, so you got soaking wet when you go out. To sit inside is hard to do when you are in a town. I have been thinking of finding work here, but it does not look too promising. As a matter of fact, there are too many workers here of all sorts so I think it is best that I go back to Kingsburg again. We plan on going out to some of the exhibits today on leaving and most likely will get soaked again.

December 16

We are now in Kingsburg and live in a so-called "Tank house", a house with a water tank on the top, on the second floor is a scrap room. We were out to see where the exhibits are going to be. Most of the buildings are almost finished. The Swedish building was at least finished on the outside, more about the exhibits another time, because I hope to see all of it at least once. The exhibits will start 20 February 1915 and be open for the whole summer.

I hope to get work here in Kingsburg and if I don't, I guess that I will live anyway. I had a letter from my brother the other day. He writes that they are busy where he is and here in the promised land a man cannot find anything to do. 2000 people come to San Francisco every week that need work, but where will they find it?

I sold a dozen wash machines in Fort Ross, but before they got there, the mill shut down, so not one worker got his machine. I left them in Cazadero and now I have written and asked that they be sent to Kingsburg. If I ever get them sold, the earnings will not be so big that they cannot be counted.

December 23, 1914

Now I have become such a bad person that I can hardly look at myself in the mirror. I planned on buying a new suit for Christmas, and went in before noon and bought one and now tonight when I went to pick it up I could not get it without money. That is the first time in my life that I have tried to buy a suit on credit and also the first time I was not able to buy on credit, so I must have shrunken considerably in people's respect. Now I will have to look like a shabby fellow for Christmas and the Sunday's to come, but it can happen sometime that I can work myself up again as creditworthy.

December 24

Since the last time I wrote, I have had an occasion to avoid "poor relief" for a while. I saw my cousin T-N in the morning and told him that I could not get a suit from L-T. T-N went with me to the other tailor here in town and there I easily got a suit. Later Christmas Eve I went to L-T and bought a couple of handkerchiefs, just to show him that I was trusted in other places beside his. He was so disappointed that he just stared at the floor.

In the morning, I'm going to prune some grapevines for painter Johnson, and later when he gets some painting work, I will help him with that. We celebrated Christmas three days this year. Since Christmas came on a Friday this year Gov. Johnson issued a decree that the whole state of California would celebrate the day after Christmas this year too.

It rained here in Kingsburg a little just before we came, but it has not rained since. It has been fairly beautiful here. A little foggy sometimes, but nothing to talk about for this time of the year.

January 10, 1915

The sun shines bright from a clear sky. The oranges are just now ripe and the temperature is about 50°. We are pruning in my vineyard and when we will get any money, only the Lord knows. If a man works hard and does not get a back ache, he can earn $2.00 a day, for 10 hours' work. The times I have had a painting job, I earned $3.00 a day for eight hours, but it is not often a man gets work in his trade. Paint can be bought in any hardware store, so the farmers can do their own painting. Here, there is an overflow of tradesmen in all trades, so if someone wants to build a house, five or six builders, underbid each other for the job. When the lucky one gets the job, he at once has several painters around him that want to paint. One that works the cheapest gets the job, and the painter boss can get as many helpers as he wants, and there are plenty. They do not have to serve an apprenticeship like you do in Sweden or to show a certificate. All they have to do is say they can, and then they can start.

If I had steady work here like I had in Sweden and only $2.00 a day plus food, I could have had between two and $3000 saved, but it is seldom a person gets work. By rights, if one prepares his own food, it will still cost about $3.00 a week for food.

There is much pruning to do here in the winter, and the Japanese do most of that, because they can do it cheap and still earn $3–4.00 a day. They usually prune poorly, but it does not matter, just so that they are a Jap. If one wants to lay and crawl on your knees and be the same kind of idiot as one of them, you can get all the work you want. Soon, two or three months pruning will be done and then it will be slow again. If by some means I can get there, in the Spring I will go to Alaska and stay for the summer. By the way, there are 16 states in the union that forbid intoxicating drinks.

January 14, 1915

We were out this afternoon asking for work but did not find any. There are mostly Swedish farmers here, us they won't hire because we are not " God's children", but the slant eyed little devils from Japan get more work than they can handle. They worship idols and are more faithful than we are after all. Yes, those are the kinds of Swedes we have here. I am ashamed that they are my countrymen.

I have worked a whole week now there is more to be done. First off, I prepared two rooms, and as soon as I was done with them I started working with Painter Johnson. I dug a ditch the first two days for $2.00 a day and then later, took up the paint brush, so now I get $3.00 a day. We are in the process of painting a schoolhouse about 15 miles from here. First, I ride my bike for 3 miles and then we ride with Johnson in his automobile. We leave Johnson's place at 7:30 and get to the school house at 8 o'clock. Yes, if the farmers come to me now and want me to work, I am busy, but in a few weeks, I will be out of work again.

The Schoolhouse

It has rained a whole week now. There is a woman in Kingsburg tonight that is a hypnotist. Should be interesting, but when you don't have any money you may just as well stay home.

February 7, 1915

I was down in Kingsburg last night and saw what it was like to be hypnotized. The money I borrowed from a friend. I never thought that there was such a wonderful power. The operator was a woman about 30 or 35 years old. First, she hypnotized seven people, one at a time and had them do all kinds of crazy things, like eat strawberries from the floor, scratch their heads, take off their clothes and scratch all over their bodies and I can't count all the things that they did. The ones that did not want to come up on stage she hypnotized where they sat on the benches. They only had to place their hands on their knees and be serious and look at her. She then told them several times that they were sleepy, and soon, they were all asleep. She then went down and said it was cold. Right away they started to freeze, stamp their feet and pull their collars up over their ears. She said," it is terribly cold, 30° below zero, but follow me to a warmer room". She then took them up on the stage and had them sit on the edge (there were seven men) and told them that they were roosters. Right away they start crowing and flapping their arms like roosters. She then gave them each a stick and told them that they were fishing on the river bank. It was impossible to keep from laughing when they cast out their lines, pulled in fish and took them off the hooks, all in thin air. Later, she had them sell a fish, they went down into the audience and hollered out that they had fish for sale. A few of them that spoke Swedish and English said, "come on, be a sport and buy fish" and so on.

She then had them look in one direction and laugh and when she had them look in the opposite direction, they were sad. If they had never laughed so unrestrained before, they stopped in the middle of their laughter and became sad. The last thing she did was to hypnotize a boy into being stiff. They then laid him between two benches, his head on one and his feet on another. They then laid a stone on his stomach that weighed 306 pounds. A man then came and pounded the stone into three or four pieces. She hypnotized 14 people at one time and if I should count up all that she did, it would take me all day, so now I will stop.

February 20, 1915

The big exhibit opened in San Francisco today and if the weather there is the same as here, they are going to get wet. I have worked the whole week, three days pruning grapes and two days painting. On the three days I earn $4.00 and on the two days I earned $6.00. I should go out and paint today, but it is raining too hard.

To pick potatoes is very hard work on your back, but to pruning grapevines is 10 times worse. I plan on taking any kind of work I can get in the future. If possible, to get enough money to go to Alaska in the Spring. They are going to build a new railroad there this summer, so I think there will be plenty of work. I am not going up in the forest anymore.

That wash machine business that I thought I would get rich on, went with David's hens under the ice. I left the last two dozens of them in a hardware store at Christmas and they have only sold three machines. I sold two dozen myself last fall.

March 16, 1915

I have had some work over winter, about enough to keep myself alive. Yes, isn't it a shame that a man should be satisfied if he earns enough for food, after he came here to earn a fortune. The rainy season is over now. We have sunshine every day and it is quite warm.

Albrekt

April 9, 1915

It was exactly 5 years since I came to Kingsburg and today is the 10th. I was in Kingsburg yesterday and listen to a skillful violinist, a Dane by the name of Skovgaard. He appeared in the New England Church. He was in Kingsburg two years ago but I did not get to see him then.

When he came on the stage (apologizing) that it was in a church, though it was more like an opera house, the people applauded. He bowed 2 feet forward, further he could not, because his stomach was in the way. He looked like he weighed about 300 pounds or more. He travels all over the world. His violin cost $13,000 and is over 200 years old. He travels in the company of two beautiful women, one an over-stiff piano player, and the other an opera singer.

If you thought of it more, he could have made a better entrance, but with his normal Danish accent he made a little speech. He spoke distressful English. He mixed in so much Danish, that it sounds like he has a big lump of porridge in his throat, and then he began to play.

What glorious tones he could draw out from his old violin. It was so quiet in the church that you could hear your watch tick. One could hardly believe that his clumsy fingers could move so swiftly over the strings. You could hear the wind murmur, the Nightingale singing, and the waters as it slaps against the cliffs. One heard the thunder's adjusted boom and the rain and hail splattering against the windowpane. At the end of the quiet after the storm, mild caressing tones. One felt as if he was being lifted by unseen hands, floating in space far from earthly life, to more blissful surroundings.

One by one the enchantment is broken and the bow taken from the strings, and the audience applauds with ecstasy and rapture. (I did not hear any foot stamping or whistling that is usually done here). Shovgaard bows a few times, 2 feet over, and then leaves the stage. The next number was the famous opera singer, followed by the piano player and then we heard Shovgaard again. Among the other songs he played were "Du Gamla du Friska" – –"He is a Second Old Bull". The last he played was "Home Sweet Home" and then we went home.

April 17, 1915

It is Saturday afternoon. I am at home waiting for man to come and get two buggies that I have painted this week. I have painted seven now, and it can happen that I will get more to paint in the future. When I get paid for the last three, I will have $50 in my pocket. I would like to go to Alaska this summer, and if I can earn enough money, I would like to go as far as Nome, but the fare for the cheapest class there cost $54.20, so if I am to go there, I will need at least $100.00. It could happen that I can get to Douglas in Southern Alaska. The fare there is only $20.00.

I will probably go to Frisco in the near future and when I get there I will decide where I will steer my course. I only charge $7.00 to paint a buggy. I used to charge $10, but there aren't many that do that, said the big shot, when he sold under the wholesale prices.

April 23

Last night I was in the New England Methodist Church. There you can at least have it a little pleasant. The church is built in the style of an opera house and it does duty for that too. The church was built last winter. Most of the work they got for nothing. I was there and painted for half a day. There are about 20 families that belong to the congregation and they have the finest church in Kingsburg. It cost about $20,000. There is a stage like in a theater and the floor slopes toward the stage so that everyone can see.

There was a concert and songs by Julia Forsblad and her siblings. She sang English songs and then later sang Swedish folk songs, the sort that you hear in the theaters in Sweden. The audience applauded and gave her flowers and then the minister took up a collection for her. Miss Forsblad is a native of Kingsburg, she has a beautiful voice. Pretty girls, that, we have plenty of, here in Kingsburg. Here you can see genuine Nordic beauty with lily white complexions and gold blonde hair and also nice black silky locks and a complexion of mashed lingon and milk with dark blue dreamy eyes. Most girls that are born here do not use so much powder and false hair as the ones that come here from Sweden, but these beautiful roses and lilies are just show bred for the boys of Kingsburg. They never go together and have no amusements except for a "social". (A gathering of young people with old people as chaperones), and also the minister among them, not to be forgotten. A social that begins with prayer and ends with one's best thanks, coffee drinking, nonsense and other unsatisfactory amusement.

I have seen Sunday school children from 5 years old to 30. It very seldom happens that anyone marries outside of their church, therefore, the disagreement between the societies become too great.

April 29

It is raining today. It has not rained this time of the year for nine years. The temperature is low for this time of the year. It is only 59° and we normally have between 90 and 100°. It looks like it will be a very good year for the fruit.

The times are unusually poor and if we get a Democratic administration next election, it will be best for America to knock the dust off of its feet, but I am certain that we will get a Republican president next time.

May 8, 1915

Yesterday the Germans sank the Lusitania. That's the boat I came over here on, so I won't be able to go home on that boat.

There are some that are successful here in the United States. There was a boy that came to Kingsburg about same time as I. He came on the same boat as I did, but got to Kingsburg a week before I did. He has earned $300 as a laborer that he has loaned out at 8 or 9% interest, now he is going to become a citizen. He went to school in Fresno last winter. He is from Stocknaryd in Smaland. There are not many that do as well as he has.

May 10, 1915

I have never in my whole life seen such a worthless person as the farmer that manages this place. He has two horses, 30 or 40 hands and 75 to 100 chicklings and if I was not here today they would have died of thirst and hunger. Sometimes when he makes believe that he is in a hurry, he comes about 8 o'clock and leaves before it gets dark, but most of the time he comes at 10 o'clock and leaves before noon. He then comes back at 3 o'clock and stays until dusk. Sometimes he does not come for several days, but now that he has hens and chicklings, he comes every day, except for today. I thought all day that he would show up some time, but to my shame I have not bothered with his hens and horses until now. They almost ate me up when they finally got food and water, but if he does not come in the morning, what will happen then? When Calle and I leave here--- dead chickens, laying all over, and more.

The man I mentioned before is a Swede, born in this country. He is an original, for example, he could charge us rent for living here. A year ago last winter the boys pruned the vines. They were supposed to get $45 for that work but that payment he did not mention anything about.

Grapevines

Grapevines

May 15, 1915

Calle and I left Kingsburg yesterday afternoon with our knapsacks tied onto the handlebars of our bicycles. We went to Fresno and stayed overnight. We left Fresno today at 6:20 in the morning and came to Chowchilla at 11:30 and had lunch. We had ridden 40 miles. Up until now we have had good roads, but that soon changed. We started out on a road that was under construction. Sometimes we had to walk, that was about 5 or 6 miles. We had a good road until we came to Merced and a state highway that runs through the whole state. It is constructed of cement with oil and gravel on top. It is just like laying a carpet on a cement floor, hard and yet soft. I had to fix my front tire in Merced later, when we got onto the newly graveled road between this place and Merced, the front tire went flat again. I went into a gas station and had it fixed, but when we left, it went flat in another place before I got on to ride. Then there was nothing else to do but stay here while Calle went on alone to Turrlock. I plan on taking the train to Stockton in the morning and meet Calle there. Later, we will take the boat to San Francisco tomorrow night. I have to pay $.50 for a very poor room here.

I almost wish that someone would be so kind as to steal my bicycle tonight so that I don't have to have any more trouble with it. They carry bicycles for free on the trains here, but even though...

Getting bicycle fixed

May 18, 1915 San Francisco

It is best that I start where I left off. I came on the train from Atwater at 7 o'clock Sunday morning to Stockton. I was out and listened to the Salvation Army band play and sing on the street and also preach. I went to a park and sat down outside of the church. A man came out of the church. When he went through the church porch he dipped his fingers in a bowl of water that was there and made a cross on his fore head, then his mouth, put on his hat and then went out. A Catholic Church I thought! Later I saw a few people, alone, come to the church, and they all dipped their fingers in the water bowl and did the same cross technique before they went in.

I took the opportunity and went in when no one would see me (I figured that if they saw that I did not make the sign of the cross, they would think that I was not a devout Catholic and would not let me into their holy shrine). I went up to the balcony and sat down. The church was so fine that I won't even try to describe its appearance. It was half dark. In front of the altar was a well-done painting of St. Mary in the middle and some other figures on each side of her. There were also paintings of saints, beautifully painted, glittering of gold and diamonds. In front of the paintings and statues, candles burn spreading a flickering mystical light that fought with the dominance in the church. On the pulpit stood a middle-aged man. He wore a white cloak, and his head was shaved except for thin band around his head. When he preached it sounded like someone reading a lesson and talking to himself. I did not understand a word he said. After carrying on for a while he left and did not appear again.

Later, another clergyman came and officiated the altar's duties. He was beautifully dressed and carried a staff that glittered and shone. There were four boys or girls by the altar with all sorts of duties. Sometimes they kneeled, sometimes they sat on a sofa, or stood still, or walked around ringing bells and so on. Sometimes the priest faced the people, and sometimes the altar. The only thing I understood was the "Pater Noster". When he spoke Latin sometimes the people kneeled, or stood or sat. I did not kneel. When they took up the collection, I did not see anyone put anything into the collection plate.

I met Calle and his brother at noontime. We went on a boat at night with San Francisco as our destination. We got there in the morning and spent the whole day at the exhibits. We were in the Swedish building a while. That was very nice, but I won't try to describe everything we saw there. Everything between times was genuine Swedish. There were beautiful oil paintings, and a portrait of Gustav V, there were boats done in miniature, and also locomotives and more, also there were weapons from Husqvarna, motorcycles and sewing machines unsurpassed work from Eskilstuna, Alfa Laval separators, electric motors, and bowls and hammers, busts of Sweden's most foremost men and women, telephones and much more. The walls were papered with fabric and the floors were covered in thick carpets that deaden the sound of footsteps.

Now this book is full, so I will have to wait a while until I can write again.

END OF BOOK 4

BOOK 5

Ft. Ross

May 23, 1915

We are in Fort Ross again. When we left here last fall, I thought that I would never come back here again. I now have a real daybook that I bought in San Francisco for $.50, but the pen is poor, along with the hand, that I cannot use.

May 24, 1915

There was so much to see at the exhibition. We were just there one day, so we did not get to see too much. We were in the Palace of Fine Arts. I think that this is the finest building in the whole place. It was full of nice paintings, but it was impossible to see all of them in such a short time. We looked for the Swedish paintings, since Sweden has seven or eight rooms there. It is odd how the word Sweden has the power to caress a Swede when he is far away from his cherished Motherland. My heart beat with love and pride for my Motherland when I saw the interest the Americans had when they looked at the beautiful winter landscapes, flower rich meadows and glittering lakes. There were paintings by Bruno Liljefors, Carl Larson, and others. There was a very fine painting of King Gustav. I thought it was strange that there were no paintings by Anders Zorn. Everything is not finished yet, but I hope to spend three or four days here this fall, if I am still here. I think that a person should go to such an exhibit alone, so as to stay in one place as long as you like without being hurried along.

May 25, 1915

When we were in Frisco the last time we went to see a few theaters. The last night we went to the Orpheum. The tickets cost from $.10 to $1.00. That is one of the finest theaters in town. The first thing that we saw was Chinese acrobats. I have seen many acrobats, but none that were as good as these young boys from Manchuria in China. I can't explain everything they did, but there were two of them that hung by their pigtails and sat on chairs with a table between them and drank beer, all this while being hung by their pigtails. We also had the pleasure of seeing, and hearing the world's two oldest singers. The bass was 76 years old and the tenor was 84 years old. They both sang exceptionally well. The curtain went up and down 11 times, and each time there was something new. Everything was good, the best I have seen otherwise, but why can't they have just one show and do it well, but Americans want so much at one time! The theater here is like the food, you can get many kinds at one time, but it is neither salted nor peppered.

I think that the above-mentioned is somewhere between a theater and a circus. It lasted for three hours. Just think if we could see a play that lasted three hours. The only thing I have seen that is very good are Chinese movies that were nine rolls long and lasted three hours. I have not been to a single theater where they don't show movies as well as a stage show. If they showed only half a roll, I think that would be enough.

May 30, 1915

It is Sunday morning, the temperature is 52°F and the boys have gone down to the shore to fish and pick abalone. The tide is at its lowest ebb that it will be all month. The sun is shining from a high blue sky. The wind is calm now but by afternoon the wind can blow hard enough to blow you over.

I am thriving well here. We live in a big cabin with three rooms in an attic. We are 10 or 12 Swedes here and the others are Americans mostly old men. The one that is the night watchman can hardly stand by himself. He is very rickety. Petterson has a new partner in place of Ochenden. Fowl is still here, but he does not have anything to say.

During the day, we are building a railroad out to the forest. I work with a pick and shovel. It is boring work but you have to trust that the mill will soon start, and then you will get a better job. The food is good. The kitchen is run by a German and his wife, with a boy from Brazil. His language is Portuguese and he speaks very little English. He got $60 a month all year round in Brazil. That's more than he can get here.

It's hell when a person like me that has a trade is forced to go and work in camps like this, but either that, or have nothing to do. In San Francisco a man can't get a job for money whether he has a trade or not. If I stay here the whole summer I can save $200-$250 and more than I can do in the camp, but you can't say that much in town. Most of the men stay here in the sawmill all summer and work, go down to some town in the fall, and stay all winter without working. When Spring comes they are all broke and then have no other choice than to go back to the forest. A man can thrive better here than in Fresno with its heat, you don't have to be fried here. I think it is about 90 or 100 degrees Fahrenheit in Kingsburg right now, that is hot enough for anyone. I am going to stop writing now and half-sole my boots instead. Here you have to be a shoemaker, tailor and washerwoman all in one, but that is how life is here in the camp.

June 6, 1915

It is foggy and quite chilly today between 60 and 70°. We are in the process of building a railroad and expect to have it finished this week. We still get good food but the man that runs the boarding house is a real cheapskate. The other day we got only one egg each for breakfast, and the cook told us that the man sold the other eggs the day before. However it was, Manley heard about the eggs and went into the cookhouse and lectured the cook, and then the cook quit, so then Manley went to the timekeeper and told him to send for some Chinese to cook for us. But "Pella" went to the cookhouse and asked the cook to stay and then gave Manley a real good lecture, so now I think that the cook will keep his skin on, at least for a few days. The fog is getting thicker and the chill is still in the air, but there is no wind.

June 13, 1915

We have beautiful weather today the most beautiful since I came here. The first Sunday it rained, the second the wind was strong enough to blow you over, and last Sunday we had fog, and today it is sunshine and calm, with a temperature of 70° in the forest.

We were out on a dairy farm that is about five minutes from here. It is a big farm with 70 cows. We were in the creamery and could drink as much cream as we wanted. This is a very fine place for a dairy farm. It is never too hot nor is it ever too cold, and the animals can go outside all year round.

The boys have been down to the beach today and gathered abalone, so I think we will have abalone soup for lunch today. On the farm, they had a big Delaval separator that was made in New York. Why don't they have a Swedish invention that is made in Sweden?

June 20, 1915

We finished the railroad Friday and Friday afternoon they tested it. They came up a passably steep hill all the way up to the first "donkey" but then there was such a sharp bend that they could not go over it. They had to go back down and when they came to where it was the steepest, the brakes did not hold and the locomotive went down the hill out of control. We were about 10 or 12 people that were riding on the donkey and among us was Herman Petterson, the boss. When the locomotive started to run away, everyone jumped off except "Red" a one eyed, redhaired Irishmen with the surprising presence of mind and no fear of death who stayed on the locomotive, and was finally able to get the brakes to hold to stop the locomotive and saved it from being wrecked. Some of the other boys and myself watched the scenario unfold from one of the donkeys. Yesterday we changed the sharp bend, but the train still could not get through it, so now we are going to take up the rails and put them in another place. Petterson is still here, and he thinks that if we can change the rails in two weeks, then we will do good.

We were down at the beach today rolling in the waves. The water was ice cold and the sun was shining and it was a nice day.

Midsummer's day 1915

I have now been in this land six Midsummer Days and spent them all in the forest. I don't think I ever came home so dirty as I have this night. We worked on the railroad today. There was soot and ashes that hit you in the face with a speed of 35 or 40 miles an hour, so tonight I looked more like a blind chimney sweep than a person that was celebrating Midsummer. It is 7:55 and getting so dark that I can hardly see the lines on the paper, so I just lit the lamp. The days are not as long at Midsummer as they are in Sweden, but then they are not as short at Christmas time as they are in Sweden.

There were three men that got laid off today, and three that quit, so the ones that are left are working real hard so that they won't get laid off too.

July 5, 1915

Now the big holiday is over. We went up to Seaview yesterday morning but could not get our checks cashed into hard cash. The saloon keeper that used to cash our checks sent some to San Francisco and got them back because they did not get the money for them. I had $35 in gold, so I loaned the boys money so that they could get drunk and take a bottle of the wretched whiskey with them as a supply when they work in such a place as this.

When we got home they were at each other's throats but there is a good guy here by the name of Eugene Felton that kept them from fighting. He quieted down a lot of trouble just to save the boys from getting black eyes.

Today after we ate breakfast some went to work but all of us Swedes and some of the others stood outside of the cookhouse. In a while Petterson came and asked if we were all sober. Then Gust, a big German, said "everybody is sober except me". Gust then took on himself to say that we were not going to do any more work until we knew that we are going to get paid.

He showed Pella a letter that came from the Italian bank in San Francisco that he had with him from Seaview, that said that they would not pay on the checks so now we are not going to do any work until they set it right again. It is very annoying with North Coast Lumber. Maybe we will have to leave here without money again. I wonder how it will end.

I hope everything will be okay so we get our money and stay here all summer.

July 15, 1915

I see that I left myself in a predicament since I last wrote so I now better write and say that things are brighter. We did not work for one and a half days. The whole trouble was that Mr. Cutting went on a trip and there were no checks in the office with his signature. Now we got good bank checks and are certain to get our money.

Once in a while everything goes crazy here. The bosses building the railroad don't understand anything and Petterson who could always lead and work with the men is not himself. Everything is crazy. Pella is 67 years old and his wife is only 24 years old. He does not talk well of being married in his old age.

When they drive on the railroad with the train the rails sometimes spread out and derail the locomotive, then they have to stop and get it back on the rails. Some places we had to take up the rails 5 and 6 times and then put them down again.

July 17, 1915

We now have a midday rest and since I work at home now in the mill, I got to rest at noon. Mr. Cutting from San Francisco honored us with a visit for a few days. He had a little talk with us about the cause for the trouble on the 4th. First, after we ate, he treated us to cigars then Mr. Cutting stood up and talked about the war, and then about how hard the times are in the shortage of work. He said that the misunderstanding on the 4th had diminished the reputation of North Coast Lumber Company as well as him and Mr. Petterson. He said that Inos, the saloon keeper was their worst enemy and that we should not go there and throw our money away. If we had to have any stimulation, we could take it home with us. Among other things he said that he would set up a few pool tables here, and the food would be the best that could be had, and at last he said that each and every one of us should consider him their personal friend and come to him when they had any problems. I have never heard an employer talk like that before and I believe that he means what he said. Henry Cutting is a stout attractive appearing middle-aged man, with an optimistic not easily excited temperament.

July 25, 1915

It has been foggy for over a week now and strangely enough we have sunshine. The railroad is now finished. I have not had to work on it for over a week now. I have been home doing carpenter work but now that is done so I don't know what I will do tomorrow. It can happen that the mill will start in the morning or Tuesday.

August 4, 1915

"From a little spark came a big fire". That we have just seen proof of. There is and has been a big forest fire. We were out all night and just got home this morning. Six boys went out in the morning and last night they came to get more help. We were just ready to go to bed, when we got the order to go out and camp near the fire. We walked 6 miles up steep hot and dusty hills until we came to the place we were to work. We set backfires a half-mile from the big fire so that when it reached our fires it could not jump over, because it had already burnt. There are steep hills in Pine Ridge, Fresno County (where I was in 1910) but they are much worse here. The fire started because a drunk Italian came home and was careless in starting a fire and burned his cabin down. The fire then spread about 20 miles around it. 4 or 500 men have been out trying to put out the fire. Today they are sending for soldiers from San Francisco, and 250 are coming from Santa Rosa. When we came home the forest was on fire here too, but they managed to stop it. The fire burned up a value of 65,000 pine trees and 4000 oak trees that went up in smoke.

August 6, 1915

It is over a week now that we started to saw and today all of the machines are going. I am not working because Herman's brother, who drives the locomotive, was disturbed with Herman. He went here for a few days threatening to quit, so now there is another driver on the locomotive. Then A–hole started to work rolling boards out in the lumberyard. I then had to leave my job as a carpenter, and be partners with A-hole. A few more men came in yesterday, but instead of taking one of them to roll boards out in the yard, and one of them take a job as carpenter and I had to continue rolling out boards. There are five different kinds of lumber that are marked as to what they are used for. They are marked for quality, best to the poorest. They are stacked according to with length and thickness. In order to read and stack the boards in their proper pile, you have to move the heavy rollers back and forth many times. I would've been satisfied with this job if I had a better partner. This man is more of a hindrance than a help, he just stood in my way when I unloaded the boards. When I tried to take boards off he held onto them and when he should've held back, he pushed the boards or couldn't tell the difference between the marks on them. Accordingly, I have had many occasions to break out in anger. I thought of quitting, but that if I could not get another job here, I would have to go back to Kingsburg in the heat and work for a farmer.

After I had lunch I went up to the cabin and told the boys that I hurt my back and would not be able to work in the afternoon and maybe not in the morning either. I told him that I hurt my back pulling too hard on a load of boards to get them started on the rollers. I was promised a job up on the conveyor belt measuring and writing down how many square feet have been sawn in the day. If more workers come, then I will get a nice job like that. More men are supposed to come tomorrow or Sunday, then we will see if they keep their word.

August 6-- 5 o'clock

Sitting here by my window, I have a full view of the lumberyard. When I look out the window I can see A-hole and J.S Gustavson (the carpenter helper) for a partner, and can see how J. (A nice boy from Smaland) is unloading boards by himself. His helper is just standing there watching.

I just heard that the forest fire covers a 60-mile area and that there are 1500 men fighting the fire and now it is finally under control.

August 10, 1915

There isn't much that happened since Friday. On Saturday, I went to Fort Ross and we went on the wild ocean in a small sailboat to measure the depth to see how close to shore a big boat could get. We had fine weather when we started out, and after we were about 2 miles out from the mill, the waves started to surge and a strong wind came up. We took down the sail. The captain and one other went into the dinghy and the engineer and five of us stayed on the big boat. We had a line between the boats and started to row slowly but the wind gets stronger. We soon found out that would not work so we all got into the big boat and tried to sail home. The wind and waves kept up and on top of that a heavy fog formed, so that we did not know where we were and where we were sailing to. The boat was thrown back and forth by the huge waves. All of a sudden, the mast broke and the sail was torn in pieces. The fog at last lifted, and we found ourselves a mile out from shore and a mile south of the mill. We now had to muster all our strength and row to shore and not be thrown onto the cliffs and stones and land without the boat being broken apart. We all waded to the shore in water up to our knees. When we got home the mill was so badly damaged that we could not work for a few weeks. We went to Stewards Point to get boxcars and came home today at noon. It is 18 miles between Stewards Point and here. We brought back 3 cars and there are 3 left. I am not working this afternoon and it looks like there's not much to do. Two of the Swedish boys and an old American quit yesterday.

August 19, 1915

I have now been here three months and I think that I will be leaving here soon. I do not like this job of driving boards out in the yard. The redwood is full of water and the juice is poisonous. If you get a sliver in your hand and don't get it out right away, your hand will swell up. When you handle the boards, your hands get sore, black, swollen and cracked. We now have sunshine in the afternoon, as a rule it is damp cold fog. Up until now we have had very nice weather.

The boss out in the lumberyard is a bit cocky. One time the other day after we worked hard for three hours straight, we took a break between loads. I sat down and rolled a cigarette, then this 25-year-old boss came and told me that it would look better if I stood up, among other things. I remember in 1912 when I sat half the time and still got $65 a month, and I didn't cry, I will soon leave anyway.

August 23, 1915

I have just quit here and I'm going to San Francisco in the morning. The three months I have been here I have put on more weight than in any other summer, owing to the food and nice climate. I now weigh 163 pounds. The temperature is almost always the same night and day, about 60°. We are two that have quit now. We are thinking of getting a job in one of the seed warehouses around Frisco.

August 31, 1915 Crockett, California

We rode with a German farmer in his farm wagon to Cazadero Train Station, where he was going anyway. He demanded two dollars apiece from us and I told him that it was shameful of him, especially since I had opened all the gates for him, but he insisted on being paid.

We stayed in Frisco a few days and saw the exhibits, and then later went to Crockett, a place that lies on the Bay about 30 miles from San Francisco. In a stretch of 3 miles, there is a sugar factory, a blast furnace and two corn warehouses out on the Bay. I worked with the Grangers warehouse on Saturday and helped load a Danish boat. It was hard work, but you could rest 20 minutes every hour. The pay was $.55 an hour and for seven hours work I will get $3.90 on Saturday.

I went to the California warehouse yesterday to ask for a job. About 9:30 Pat O'Brien the boss asked me if I knew how to staple sacks. I can try was my answer. He motioned to me with his hand to follow him. We met a man with a wheelbarrow. Pat then said that I should go with this man and show him what he should do, so I went and got a wheelbarrow, but then Pat came and said, "I did not tell you to work". I then went home, and decided that I would not go back to him again.

September 1, 1915

I went to the sugar factory today but could not get a job. We were about 20 people that went home. Had I gone there yesterday, I might've been able to stay.

It has been hot here the last few days but now it's cool and nice. If I don't find something to do soon, then I won't be able to stay here much longer. I don't know when I will get my money for the seven hours I worked on Saturday. Had I known that I would be without work, I would have gone on the Danish boat to Copenhagen.

September 2, 1915

We went down to "California and Hawaii Sugar Refining Company" today and that was the same as yesterday. We were as many today as yesterday. It was the same, no work, so they all went home with a sour expression on their faces.

It is surprising how American chefs can shame good food. We were in a restaurant today and ate. We got a little oatmeal and separated milk in an oblong plate about 6 inches long and 3 inches wide. After that you had a choice between beefsteak, eggs and bacon. The eggs were almost raw so I took the beefsteak. The steak was about 10 inches long and 6 inches wide and a half inch thick. It was almost all raw. I thought it was more fitting for a tiger than a man, since it was cooked without onions, pepper or salt. It looks like this book could be good medicine for someone that has America fever. I, myself am almost cured.

September 4, 1915

I have a bad cold and feel downtrodden. I have been here over a week and only worked seven hours. I think I will go to San Francisco in the morning and see the exhibits for a few days, and then go to Kingsburg. There is no point in staying here. I was in a shoe store and asked the owner if he could cash a check for me, but he said no even though I showed him that I had $50 in the Canadian Bank of Commerce in San Francisco. I think I could thrive here if I could find something to do

September 7, 1915 San Francisco California

I was at the exhibits yesterday but it was not a good day to go there, because it was the first Monday in September, United States Labor Day. To try and describe everything to be seen at the exhibits is impossible. It would take up the whole book.

I went to a dentist today to have a gold crown put

on. He wanted $7.00 for it, and in other places they want between $3–5 dollars. I told the dentist I would be back at 2 o'clock. I hope that he didn't wait too long. I am going to stay here one more night, and then go to an employment office in the morning and see if I can get a job. I can't stay here much longer.

This afternoon I have seen the world's most skillful engraver's last work. He engraved the whole Lord's Prayer on the head of a straight pin, made of gold with a flathead a 16th of an inch in diameter. You could not see it with the naked eye, but through a microscope you could read it from beginning to end. It took three years to do the engraving and was done by a Swede by the name of H.A. Klinke. He lives here in Frisco. I saw this art work in a show on Market Street and think it was odd that they did not have it in one of the exhibits.

September 10, 1915

Now I am back here. I could not find any work in Frisco that suited me, so I thought I would go to Kingsburg but then I know how it is there, so why go there? I tried four different places today to get a job painting, without luck and am going to try one more time. I am going about 200 miles north of here to Richvale, a Swedish settlement. They grow mostly rice there.

A friend of mine and a Danish boy were there last fall and got work as soon as they got there. The pay was $2.00 a day with room and board so you did not have to drag blankets and mattresses with you. Out of the $85 I had when I left Fort Ross, I now have $34 left, so I spent $51 and in the morning the train fare will cost $6.00 to Richvale.

Maybe when I get there I won't get any work, then I will have to go back to Kingsburg and then there won't be very much left of my $34.

So now it looks like when I quit Petterson's Mill, I was a genuine ass, when I think how much value the $50 I let go would've been in Sweden. But I am not the only one here that is going like this. There are many that are seven times worse off than me. I didn't spend any money on booze like most of my landsmen do. Besides, I have $70, but when I will get them I don't know. There are about 10 here that manage without Swedes. The trouble with me is that once I have come to a place I can't stay. I always think that if I go here or there I will get a better job with more money. If there were no war, then there would be plenty of work. Many boats do not go out now for fear of submarines. The war has ruined everything. If it hadn't been for the war, I would've had the money I had planned on so that I could go home this fall. The next time I write I will most likely be in Richvale.

September 11, 1915

I am now in a Swedish settlement, but I have come a month too early. When Arthur was here last fall, he came in October and now I am here in the beginning of September. There is only one hotel and it is Swedish and that is where I live. The lady that runs the hotel speaks Swedish and is very talkative. She invited me for coffee this afternoon. If I can find something to do it will probably be just enough to buy food. I can't understand what I will do in this desolate place. I don't think I will be comfortable so that I have to be somewhere.

It is warm and sunny here. There is a Swedish and

English church here. I will be the priest in the Swedish church because they cannot afford a full-time priest. All of the other sects have a church together.

September 12, 1915

I have met a Swedish boy that is a carpenter and I may help him to build a house or something. It is 3 miles from here and he went out to look at it. I am bored here. I don't know anyone and it is deserted here. There are about 20 houses, two churches, two stores and one schoolhouse. The train station is a luggage van.

The temperature is 65° and for me that is just right. If I had not already had my train ticket, I could have gotten a job in Sacramento. It looks like the only way I can exist, is to work in the forest in the summer and Kingsburg in the winter.

When I came to the Lofgren boys that Arthur told me to go and see, I felt that they regarded me as a person that looked poorly, and that it was their duty to help me because I was a fellow countryman, even though I was nicely dressed and looked like a gentleman.

I did not come here to just earn enough for room and board (that I can do in Kingsburg). I came here to earn money and see what it was like here. Four years ago, there was not a single house here and now as far as you can see in every direction are rice fields with farms here and there. I saw an article in the newspaper that said that this is the richest land in California. Farms are from 160 acres to 600 acres each. Rice grows like other plants and looks like something between corn and oats, with the exception that it grows in water, so there are canals here like in Kingsburg that they flood the fields. Fields have to be level so that the water is the same depth all over. The ground looks like rich black clay and is hard when it is dry.

September 13, 1915

I rode my bicycle out to the farm where I was going to work. I met Mr. Spence by his big electric power plant. He asked me if I knew what I was to do and I said I did not. He said I could go and nail some boards on the roof. I went out to the farm and there I saw what "early life in California" was like. On the flat prairie was a four-cornered house the people lived in while it was still under construction. There were no windows or openings where windows would go. In one room where I was to work, a sick woman laid in misery and suffering. Any reasonable person could understand why I did not want to start work in that room, besides I could not find a hammer or any nails. There were only enough boards to last a few hours. There was nothing else to do but go home. Home!!! What home do I have? I am a foreigner here. I can't understand what I am doing here.

September 15, 1915

Today it is 55°F so I think the nights will be cold this Fall. I took my bicycle and rode 8 miles up to Biggs, the closest railroad station that goes South. It was not a particularly nice way to go, but since I had nothing else to do, it was satisfying.

Why on earth am I going so long without employment, traveling on trains, and living in hotels? This way I am ruining what I have worked and suffered for. The worst is that I am not getting any enjoyment from my money. I met a Turk when I rode home from Biggs yesterday. I offered him a cigarette, but he neither smoked or drank or ate all kinds of food. He ate some kinds of vegetables and only certain kinds of meat, only if you kill the animal himself. His English was very poor, but I understood the most of what he said.

September 15, 1915

It has been warm today, 84°F. I was going to take a nap today at noon, but after a while I was soaked in sweat. The food here is very good and nicely served, almost too good for me. Two lady teachers eat at the same table as me, they are so fine that I feel like a genuine Smaland farmer in "Berns Saloon".

I was promised to be able to work in the morning. I don't understand myself, if I'm in the forest, I want to be in the flat ground and the other way around. Now I wish that I had stayed in Fort Ross or gone to Kingsburg. I seem to thrive the best in Kingsburg. I even thrive in San Francisco, but I can't stay there because there it is easier to take the moon down than to get a job.

I see on page 3 of this book that I named some theaters that are not famous. They were variety theaters. When I was in San Francisco last, I saw one of the states finest theaters. They had a play from 1849 California by the name of "The Girl of the Golden West". The play had 4 actors and lasted 3 hours. That is what I like to see when I visit a theater. I forgot to mention that you do not have to be a millionaire to ride in a car in San Francisco. For $.10 you can ride through the whole town, and for $.05 you can ride up to 17th St. The trolley company does not like that and is in the process of trying to get the automobiles banned, and that could happen.

September 16, 1915

Today, after being out of work for months, I went through a worker's purgatory. I was out and did carpenter work and got a ride in an automobile to do the job. The forenoon went good, but in the afternoon, I worked on the sunny side of a wall and thought that I would melt. I drank water like an ox, and as soon as I drink a few cups it came out in the form of sweat. My mouth was always dry, and now I could not work fast enough.

In the late afternoon, I went up on the roof to nail some shingles. I slid as if I was on ice, the shingle split, the sun burned, and I forgot to nail shingles in some places. Nelson came and saw that, so he nailed them in place. On top of all of the trouble I had, I got a splitting headache from all the water I drink. I was ready to give up the whole thing and get on a boat and go to some sawmill or go to Kingsburg.

When I got in the car and took off my old wide-brimmed hat and the wind cooled my burning forehead, I felt a little energy returning and then I thought that if I give up that easy when I come across a little trouble, then I will always have trouble and in the end I will just be a tramp, so therefore I will stay here even if it is 10 times worse than at Fort Ross.

The time is 4:30 and the temperature is 90°. I see drops of sweat as big as peas dangling from my forehead in the mirror. I went outside a while but had to go in because I was losing too much blood to the insects. It is certainly uncomfortable to sit in this sweat bath, but it is better than being eaten alive by the California mosquitoes.

September 19

It is Sunday night and 87°F. I have come home from a summer outing. I will now write down my experiences of that. I was invited by the lady that runs a hotel to go with on a picnic or whatever you call it, to Durham. I rode the train from Durham and then had to wait a while until the cars came from Richvale. We then rode out to the place where this cozy afternoon entertainment was to take place. We were to have dinner out in the greenery. We came to a place that had many oak trees, struggling against the dry heat with their leaves full of dust. The ground had grass that was brown. In spite of this, this was the place that I had paid $.35 to come to. The others had driven 14 miles in their cars to come to this "Eden". When we were there, the women started to set out the food on a tablecloth on the ground. The food was good and even had an ostkaka (cheesecake). We then ate and enjoyed the food, because we were there to have a good time. We each took a part of a newspaper and sat in the cars and read, some stood and talked, laughed and had a good time. Lucky people that could have a good time. I must be bold and confess that I was bored to death. I made a comparison between such an outing here and in Smaland and came to the conclusion that it was even more boring here. We were out and had some fun. The temperature was 100°F and everyone looked like they were dipped in oil. The women took the cars and rode to a farm, and we men, took the horses and rode out to a canal to bathe. When we came back, the women were already back and then we were going to "play". We played several games that we played in Sweden when we were six or seven years old, like the cat and the rat, and others. These Swedes that are born here were having a good time, so that I, too, became involved and I, too, must have a good time. We continued playing about 15 minutes, ate supper and then rode home. The ride home was the best of all for me. I thought it rather pleasant to glide over the prairie in the evening's murmur. The sun was going down and cast a blood red shimmer on the mountain tops in the West. The air was pleasantly warm. Here and there we rode through a small stand of oaks, and then out on the open prairie again.

Summer outing

September 23

I am thriving right well now, even my career as a carpenter is doing good. Nelson is a good boss. If you do something wrong, he remains calm and shows how it should be done. He is not like some bosses both here and Sweden. They yell and scream as if you had murdered your mother and father and burned down the church, for the most minor mistake. It is odd that I cannot get a position in the trade that I have learned, and in trade that I have not learned, I can get work.

I am beginning to be known here now. All the people greet me. Two farmers have asked me if I want to work for them at harvest time, but as of now I have not decided as to who I will work for. The air is cooler now about 70° tonight.

September 26, 1915

I feel very good just now I just had a good dinner and a good smoke on top. What else can a man ask for? I think I will go and visit one of my friends this afternoon. He is a Smalander from Kronosbergsland.

I was in the schoolhouse last night. They have a meeting there every Saturday night. One room is built like a theater with scenery and a curtain and all that is needed. When we came here there was a young boy up on the stage and he talked nonsense. I said to them that if they understood Swedish that I too, could find it in my breast to go up and behave dumb too. There were about a third of them that understood the language of honor and heroes and the ones that did not understand, alleged that it would please them anyway. I went up on the stage and recited Froling's "In a Dilemma". I mentioned that some of them understood the poem and I could hear laughter here and there from the ones that did not. Today the schoolteachers expressed their sorrow that all of them did not understand Swedish.

October 1, 1915

It is as hot as the devil again today. I have a cross draft to cool off the air and it is still 100°F. I am now done with my carpenter job. I was out and harvested rice today with the method that they used in Sweden before they had scythes, namely a sickle. They still use a sickle in Japan and China today. There was too much water on the ground to go out with the reaping machine. The rice we are trying to harvest ripens three weeks before the rice that the other farmers are growing. The Land Company has tried 29 different kinds of rice to see which one grows best in the Riverdale area. I don't think they have found the right one yet.

October 20, 1915

We have finished setting up the sheaves and have started to thrash today. Work here is for two Smalanders and the pay is $2.00 a day with room and board. The work has been easy. We have not worked more than eight hours a day and sometimes only 6 or 7 hours. Now after this we will get up at 6:30, eat and then go out and work until noon. We get an hour for lunch and then go back out and work as long as you can see, about at 5:45. So far, I like this work and now I will see how it goes with the thrashing, and if I still like it, I'm going to move to a cabin and have it rent-free, but there is not much furniture, and I will have to sleep on the floor. I guess that I will have to use the floor for a table too if I want to write.

October 23 Richvale

We had a few drops of rain so we did not go out this morning but then it cleared up and we ate lunch at 11:00 and then worked until almost dark which we do every night. I am fairly tired tonight. Tomorrow is Sunday and we plan on working anyway. We have to hurry up, if possible, and get in the sheaves before the rain starts. We get up at 6:30. We are seven people in this cabin and sleep on the floor.

October 24

When I went to school, I learned that "God does not bless the Sunday worker", and today we saw the truth in that. First of all, the thrashing machine kept breaking down so that we had to stop and get it going again. Two of us broke down with our wagons, and one broke his pitchfork apart. One got a blue fingernail and one had his leg clipped off by an iron chain. I drove my pitchfork into the leg of an American. I, myself did not get away without a big sliver in my hand. The boss should be religious but he does not take it seriously because he should observe the day of rest and believe that God gives us nice weather so that we can get in the sheaves on the weekday. This rice field is owned by Mr. Spence and it is 600 acres. The owner estimates that the rice crop will bring in about 4 or $5000, if all goes well, but that is like playing the lottery. It can happen that it will not go so good, anyway, a man can be glad if he has the income to pay his expenses. Last year there was so much rain that they could not thrash until spring, so the income was likely low. So far it looks good for this year.

October 31

Last night I was at a Halloween party at the schoolhouse. I had a very nice time. The schoolhouse was completely decorated with gold and blue crêpe paper, the colors of California. We were there until 11:30 at night. Wednesday, the boss came out and told us that we had to put on a little more speed. He thought we were too lazy even though we all work the best we could. We thrashed 170 sacks in an hour and 10 minutes and if you thrashed 100 sacks in an hour, that is not bad. That is $20 an hour at $.20 a sack. Awhile later he came out with a pitchfork to help me load.

Normally a man is satisfied to take one sheave at a time and load, but in his anger, he took two and three, so to outdo him, I took four. In that way, the Dane that was up at the top of the load and stacked the sheaves became almost invisible. He was so mad that he sizzled, but he did not say anything and neither did I. But I was thinking of quitting at noon. But when we got lunch there was a fried chicken and more good food, so that I softened up my mood and figured that if the others stayed, then so would I. All 13 of us have agreed that there will be no more "speed" and to let things go their "merry way". He speeded the machine up to the extreme, but even a machine has to be handled humanely--- also the machine became so mad that it quit. It broke down midday on Thursday, and they still haven't gotten a going yet.

They had a man here from Maryville where the machine was made, but he did not understand anything about how to fix it, and now they have sent for another man and I think he will get it going, so it could happen that we will begin to work again this afternoon (it is Sunday today).

It was lucky that we left Fort Ross when we did. The sawmill burnt down and the boys that stayed there only got five dollars, so they could not leave there. The fire looks a little suspicious. I don't understand how that old mill could burn down so fast. The workers left the mill at 12:15 and everything was normal. At 12:17 they went into the cookhouse to eat. At 12:20 they all had to go down to the mill because the whole mill was on fire, but it was impossible to put the fire out. the only thing that could be done, was to save the lumberyard from that fearful element, fire. The saw was insured but for how much I don't know. Actually, it would have been better if that saw disappeared from the face of the earth. It was the dumbest saw that was ever built. It took twice as much manpower than if it had been properly built.

November 15, 1915 Kingsburg California

I am now back here in Kingsburg after being away for six months and strangely enough I am back at the same place that I was last fall when I came to Kingsburg. We really started to thrash Sunday afternoon and kept up until Sunday night and into next Sunday night, and then the thrashing was done. We were all dismissed and given our money. Later that night the boss said that he had a job for Monday if anyone wanted to do some more thrashing. The boys did not want to go out again and it was just as well, for it started to rain Monday afternoon. The rain came down harder and harder until the ground was flooded. All the rice was in except for 70 acres. Mr. Spence has 600 acres so he has a lot of rice that is still standing and rotting. He is going to have a lot of trouble to get his crop in. The last week I was in Richvale I liked it very much. We came on a better way to load. We did not load every which way, instead each person has his definite position in loading, and that way we work for 15 minutes and rested for 10 minutes. Between times we went to Oroville and look for work in the big orange groves, but came there two weeks too early. It was cold and rainy so we stayed overnight. Later we took an electric train to Sacramento and arrived in the afternoon and stayed overnight there. It was cold and rainy there too the whole time so that I caught a cold, but the day after, I took the first train to Kingsburg, but there is no work here. A man can always find enough to support himself. I worked five months when I left Kingsburg and all I managed to save is $25 and this money I intend to save and if I find something to do I will add to it.

Now I have work!!! I have worked two days for one boss and two days for my old boss that I work for last winter. Hopefully I will work every day until Christmas because all the farmers want to have everything freshly painted and nice for the big holiday.

December 5, 1915

This week I worked five and half days and could have worked the other half too if my most unpleasant incident had not happened, namely, that I had to take back the land. When I bought the land three years ago, I was a big jackass and I wonder why I did not see my big ears. I am sure they must have been a yard long. Had I always made decisions on my own judgment and not followed "good advice" so much, I may have avoided many mistakes. The first mistake was that we bought the land, the second was that we paid too much, and the third, is that we located the water pump in a place where we could only water 18 acres of our land. In all of this I have let myself be led like a mindless tool that did not understand anything and that the others could decide what was best for me.

It was planned that Knut and I would go up in the forest and earn $300 each year and that would work out fine. If I could've earned $300 a year, it would have been better to put it in the bank and draw interest, than to put it in a piece of land that would not produce any income until it was eight or nine years old, but in my unwise childish thoughts, I thought that we would keep the land until fall and then sell it. Each of us would have about $1500 in each of our pockets

I have now come to the conclusion that we paid about $500 too much, and that the land has been neglected. It should be worth $7000 but now at the highest it's only worth about $5500. When I sold the land a year ago I made the best deal since I came here if the boys could hold onto it, but that is just what they could not do. The fact is, they have no experience in farming in California. They have managed the land so poorly that they have only gotten $36 for the raisins. In money, they have only laid out $200 in the Summer and now it is Fall and they have to leave the land because they have no money to pay the debts or the interest. Now we have that to worry about, and if we can't pay we will have to do like Anderson, leave the land back to Eklund. So far, I have $646.75 invested in the land and would have to say farewell to it if I now give up the land.

There are two experienced people that have given me the advice that if I try to hold on, I will be throwing good money after bad and in the end be forced to give it up anyway. That is $200 less than we sold it for last fall and in the worst deal, knockoff $300. Anyway, I will get $200 that I paid when we bought the land. Yes, this can drive a man mad but what good would that do? No, I will take it fairly cool.

December 16, 1915

The weather is beautiful today. Bright sunshine but somewhat chilly. I'm sitting home and cooking supper though I could be out working painting a buggy. We bought meat yesterday and now it has to be cooked before it spoils. I think that if I was married my sweet little wife would be home watching the soup pot while I was out painting earning money to buy something to put in it. I do not want to tie the knot of holy matrimony here in America. The first thing is that I would never get back to Sweden, and the second is that almost all the women are spoiled so much that I would not want to marry any of them. It is understandable that there is one or the other that would be suitable to tie yourself to for life, but there are a few.

I always thought that I would go home to Sweden at Christmas 1915 with a nice fur coat, gold trappings, money and more. Had I not been so dumb as to buy that land, my dream might have happened. And if I put my money in the bank, I would have been able to take it out when I wanted plus interest.

How should I do now after my beautiful soap bubbles have broken? Should I leave my land or should I hold onto it? Yes, I will hold on, at least until the next time I have to lay out more money. In the meantime, I will try to sell it at least to save some of my money. However it goes, I must go back to "Mother Sweden" before Christmas 1916 and if nothing else, I can hire myself out on some boat to Sweden.

December 27, 1915

Christmas is over and we celebrated in full force. The day before Christmas Eve they had a Christmas party in the street right in the middle of town. A 30-foot-high Christmas tree was set up. It was a cypress that was planted 27 years ago on the edge of town. It was fully decorated with electric lights of many colors. The Kings-burg band provided the music and the schoolchildren had their little plays and more. The last was Santa's arrival pulled by a pair of ponies, and all the children from one to 12 years old got a Christmas present.

We spent Christmas Eve at Lindholm's on the invitation of the son. It was fairly nice, although the songs the boys sang were not suitable for Christmas Eve. They sang songs from the young socialist alliance songbook. We were away Christmas day for dinner and the next day we were at another place and had dinner and then Christmas of 1915 was just a memory.

A man can have a confusing life. An old man that lives in a cabin, and prepares his own food (if you can call it that) that he scrapes together, is hardly regarded as human. I can hardly be counted as "old young man" (I'm only 26 years old), but if I live and have my health and stay in Kingsburg than I can be fairly certain that in time I will attain that envious title of "old young man".

January 2, 1916

A.D. 1915 has now gathered together its predecessors and the world historians cannot show any to match it. Think how much has been sacrificed on the war's altar this past year. 1915 will stand as a dark threatening, blood dripping cloud through the coming centuries, casting a dark spot like an unchallenged showing of a higher culture that had become more brutal and heartless. It sounds almost impossible that such a thing can happen in the 1900's enlightened time. The leading powers of this devilish war on countries where culture is not the high point. It is possible for a person to love his Mother Land without having to hate other nations for example, I love my Mother Land, but I do not hate the Russian people. I detest war and hate it with all my soul along with such people that start wars for sordid winnings and those who approve of it. It is my opinion that the capitalists are the cause of this war, because they are the only ones that gain from it. They become richer every day it keeps on and where does the money come from? It will come as taxes for the poor people in now belligerent countries once the peace has ended. This money that these "Big Men" will grab comes from the parents that have a ready sacrificed their sons in the war and from invalids that have sacrificed their limbs for the Motherland.

I read in this "San Francisco Examiner" that the United States could stop this war in a month by not exporting any food or war materials to the warring nations. Why don't they stop exporting? Because egotism chokes out all noble feelings in this money feeding frenzy. Take for example, if Sven Hedin had been King in Sweden, then Sweden would have been involved in the war long ago, but fortunately there is a man sitting on the throne and not a war fanatic like Sven Hedin. Now let us leave the war and see what is happening here in peaceful Fresno County.

It has been so cold here between Christmas and New Year's that we have a half inch of snow and that has not been seen in the last six years.

I was in Fresno and welcomed the New Year. That is a night when people do very much as they please without the police interfering and the truth is, the people take advantage of that fact. They dress up in costumes so that they look like oafish buffoons. Later they go out in the street and make as much noise as they can with cowbells whistles and other lesser instruments of noise. They tie old dish pans, plowshares and whatever they can find onto the back of cars and drive around the streets. At midnight, they "shoot" in the New Year and then they go home.

This New Year's started with snow and then turned to rain. New Year's Eve I did not think that we would have any precipitation. The sky was clear of clouds and the temperature was 32° (I was unbearably cold). When we got up on 1st of January, the roof had a blanket of the whitest snow, which was later washed away by the rain. It rained the whole night and it is still raining.

January 5, 1916

I have now by grace gotten a few days of work painting but it would almost be just as well to be without, because if you have work, you have to work as though you were trying to scratch butter out of the fire.

Today we worked in a big department store in town. Johnson is getting $74 for the work when he should get $125. The painting prices have come down quite a bit here in Kingsburg. There were no less than three painters that were here today and yesterday asking for work without results. Johnson could've had one of them to work for two dollars a day but he can hire only one. On such an occasion when he has too much that must be finished at the same time, or when he has such work that one man can do it alone. I think I will hold back and not fight with them over the work a little further on.

We have 4 1/2 acres in alfalfa that is now too old, so I think that we will plow it under. My cousins want to plant oats on their part (and mine too), but I'm going to try my luck with potatoes. If it goes good, then it will make some good money, if not, then it will hardly pay for the labor and the potato seed, but if you want to win something, you have to take the chance.

January 11, 1916

I should have been out painting today, but the weather is not suitable for painting outside, it is too cold and foggy. So far, we have had more rain than sunshine in this hopeful New Year of 1916. Last night I was out and rode my bicycle and came home soaking wet, and yet I am glad, because a lot of rain in the winter is the first sign that there will be a good harvest. This morning when I got up it was 32°, so I thought that it must be about 27 outside, but it was only 32° cold. That is the coldest we have had this winter. When it rains and hails during the day and clears up in the evening, you can count on a cold night. When the sun comes up it becomes foggy and you can't see the sun.

January 17, 1916

It's raining and blustery today and between showers the sun peeks out for a while. It has been very rainy this month, more than I have seen since I came to California. It is now storming so hard that the ground is just shaking. I was just out and took in my clothes that I had hung outside to dry and they were spread all over the courtyard! We have had only two sunny days so far this January.

I was finished painting Saturday. I have already earned $69 in the fall and am at peace knowing that I did my share. It is terrible how a man has to toil here in Kingsburg, if by chance he is lucky enough to find something to do.

Today a Swedish boy is being operated on for appendicitis, one of my good friends from Hagafors in Smaland. A doctor from Kingsburg is doing the operating in his own operating room. He is a surgeon. The worst of it is, that in this land that without consideration they charge $250 for such an operation. In Swedish money it is 1000 kroner (crowns) and to think in Sweden it would cost about 5 or 10 crowns. To be sure, there is a county hospital in every county, but no one goes there if they can pay. If they can't pay, then they don't much care if the patient lives or dies. For instance, if you can pay you must say so, if you go to the county hospital. There is much that should be changed in this robber land, but the poor that would like to have it like it is in Sweden have no say and the rich could care less about such a system.

January 29, 1916

When I last wrote about the storm I did not realize how bad it was and that it could have so much power. Everywhere you go you can see trees that have been blown down, roofs blown off houses, and even some houses that were blown down. I saw on the Fresno Republican that the storm damage amounts to over $500,000. So, there you can see how much power there is in the wind when it blows so hard.

5:10 in the evening, the sun is just going down and is casting a golden glimmer on the majestic Sierra Nevada Mountains in the East which are covered with the whitest snow.

Sierra Nevada mountains surround the San Joaquin Valley in a half circle, like newly melted silver. It is nice to see nature in all her majestic beauty. Light clouds float in the sky together with the dark rain clouds. The sun went down in the dark clouds, but just as it went down, there was a crack large enough for her to cast her golden leaves on the silver topped mountains. There is a saying in Sweden that when the sun goes down and it is clear, then you will have nice weather. I hope that applies the same here because it is time that we have nice weather, at least for a few days.

January 31, 1916

My prediction of the weather has become a fact. We have not had any rain fog or frost. It was 33° in the morning and we have had sunshine since 11 o'clock. The temperature has been low because of the heavy snow up on the mountain tops. I am thinking of planting my potatoes in the morning, 1 February and maybe 1 May I can dig them up or maybe sooner.

February 4, 1916

I planted my potatoes on the first of the month. We had beautiful weather that day, sunshine and warm and fog in the morning. I cut up the potatoes a whole week before we planted them. I fertilize them with bone-meal which is supposed to be good. That way, the potato field now cost me $60 and before I can take them up it can cost twice as much. If I get a good harvest, I can take in as much as $300.

It has been beautiful weather the last few days but today it is raining. I should be out on the farm today building on my cabin but in weather like this you can't be out doing such work. The worst of it is that the lumber is laying outside and getting soaking wet and then in the summer when it gets warm and they dry out you will be able to read a newspaper through the walls. It is crazy to sit here idle when there is so much that must be done. I should sow oats, plant carrots and onions among other things, and also prune the grapes and more. If it would only hold so that a man can work. The time is 5:30. I have just read in the paper something that might be interesting to write down here. It reads as follows--- 150-year-old Indian woman died recently by the name of Mary Tecugas who belong to the so-called Tejas tribe that lives near Bakersfield California. More than 15 members of this tribe can write their age with three numbers, it is understood---. It is surprising that wild people can live so long! I have been with the same tribe up in the forest and when I learned that a man and a woman were 115 and 110 years old, I did not believe it because they did not look more than 100 at the most.

The Indians here are small in stature, are homely and they like "pionn" (whiskey). They are fairly good workers and peaceful when in a sober state. It is against the law to sell spirits to them, but it is easy for them to get it anyway. When they have had too much and are drunk, then the wildness in them appears in all its terrible nakedness. They then let out their emotions by wild howling and more. The most of the time, the women are barefooted, fat and ill formed, somewhere between a sack of hay (poorly stuffed) and an oil barrel. Even though, there are many whites among the Scandinavians that are married to "squaws" and have children with them. If a man wants to marry a squaw, he only has to go to the chief and buy one for $30, and then that affair is settled. I know a Danish man that is up in the forest, he bought himself an Indian wife and lived with her for 20 years, then he wanted to change, so he took his oldest daughter for a mate instead. That is against California law, but there is neither a prosecutor or judge. The half Indians as a rule are healthy and strong and good comrades, but have no compassion if it is needed, in particular, if they have a little of the noble grape in their marrow. It has rained all day today. I wonder how soon it will stop.

February 18, 1916

I don't feel too anxious to take the pen in my hand tonight, because I have picked twigs all day and the fingers are stiff and not suitable for holding a pen, but anyway like Nicodemus Svensson said, when you can put your feet in your own home, then it is best to confide that gratifying event in my daybook.

It took me about 2 1/2 days to build my cabin. It is 8 feet wide and 12 feet long. It is 8 feet high on one side and 7 feet high on the other. It has two windows and a door. I drew the plans and then built the cabin myself, because there was no one else that could read the plans. The weather the last few days has been excellent. I have plenty of work, so I don't have to be on the lazy side. I like working like this for myself and see how the trees are budding out. I have planted onions carrots beets and parsnips. I also have a large potato patch.

If I could only get rid of the squirrels, they look like ekorrars in Sweden, but are gray in color. Their tails are somewhere between an ekorrar's tail and a rat. They are very shy and it is very hard to get them in your gun sights. They do a lot of damage to the land wherever they are. They ate up a great deal of Anderson's raisins last fall. They dragged the paper trays down on the ground and the squirrels and the moles ate them up, or the rabbits ate the rest.

At first, I thought it was a little funny to be alone like this, but now I think it is even better than being together with someone else. At least now I can do as I like, eat what I want and be alone when I want, because it is seldom that anyone comes here. I have lived here for a week now. I moved here Friday, 11 February 1916.

I had a telephone call from Johnson eight days ago. He wanted me to work for him for a few days again but I said no because now some of the painters in Kingsburg can work for Johnson and then they won't have to go and give me dirty looks. I have plenty of work here, beside, I live 5 miles from Kingsburg and that is too far to go morning and night.

March 12, 1916

This could be the time to "sing the blues" in this book. It is three weeks since I last wrote and now I will sing of Jeremiahs lament. It was hot as hell here, I was out and walked in the vineyard. Sweat dropped off the tip of my nose as usual like clockwork. The sun burned and not a breeze could be felt. The strong light in my face loaded my face with creases and wrinkles forever. It's no wonder a man becomes old in such a climate. When I went into my cabin at noon the temperature stood at 100°. One can imagine how nice it was to make a fire in the stove to prepare food, but that wasn't enough! Hell was in that cabin-- about 100 wasps were circling around in the wildest dance, but since the hateful insects were considerate enough not to land on me, I was able to get away with just listening to their ear deafening buzzing. The next morning it was a little chilly so they could not fly and then I gave them a ticket to the happy hunting grounds. Five of them are left and they keep me company now. It is cool and nice now, it's about

80°F.

My potatoes are up now and thriving well. I also have a large garden, but now the rabbits and squirrels are having a hard time leaving it alone, so I don't think I will have much of a harvest.

March 20, 1916

We have beautiful weather today. It was nice that it rained and flooded over the dry ground. Here in Fresno County you can't get too much rain. Here we never get any rain between May 1 until usually December 1 and if there is any in between, then it is very little. My potatoes are growing and flourishing. I think I will get a good harvest if only I get a good price for them too.

March 24, 1916

Now my potatoes have frozen. They froze today just before sunrise. I was out at 4 AM and tried to make fires with old cornstalks but I could not get them to burn because it rained all week on them. I lost a lot of money that frosty night. There was no one else around here that had potatoes as fine as mine were. They would have bloomed in a few weeks had they not frozen and later they would have ripened early and I would have gotten $300 a sack or more for them. I might have gotten 200 sacks. That would have been $600. Now they will be set back a month in growing time and maybe bring one dollar a sack and yield only 100 sacks, for $100. That will hardly pay for the seed and bone meal.

Should a man cry or swear, hang yourself, or shoot yourself? NO! Take the matter as it comes. That is not the first time things have gone against me. I can console myself in the fact that they have frozen for others as well.

It is nearly a month since I last held this pen and then it was just to complain, and I think that is what it will be now too. #1-- I have a toothache. #2-- is it good to be alone in monotony? #3-- I have nothing to read for the time being. #4-- the moles are continuing to eat up my potatoes. I have put a poison gas into their holes to kill them. #5--am I brainless because I can't make up my mind whether to water my potatoes or not? #6-- will there be an un-ordinary harvest of parsnips and for #7-- and the worst-- is that Monday is the last day to pay the taxes and I have only five cents in cash.

I dug no potatoes today. The price for them is $.04 a pound so it does not pay to dig them up anymore for now. The largest are about 1 1/4 to 2 inches in diameter. In five or six weeks they will get to be 5 inches long and 2 to 3 inches thick. If I only get $.01-.015 a pound for them, then I think it is more profitable to dig them up now. It looks like it will be a good harvest of grapes this year, if only we can keep the mildew and other vermin at a safe distance, then maybe there will be a few dollars' income. Last year mildew destroyed the whole crop but this year I've spread sulfur on the bushes once already, and after a time, I will spread on some more. It's the kind of work that a man's legs get tired. To do 10 acres you have to go 10 miles in the loose dirt. The sulfur powder is put in a sack and shaken over each vine bush so that it is a dust. That is all that is needed.

My tooth is continuing to ache but I can't go to the dentist without any money. There is nothing more to do than roll a cigarette to help ease the annoyance of the pain, also, my watch has stopped. That was the eighth stumbling block.

June 4, 1916

I hardly know what to write about it has been so long since I confided in my daybook that it is high time that we talk. A few hours ago, my head was full of thoughts, but then it was so hot that I could not write and now my head is as empty as my money pouch, but I will find something.

On Wednesday, I have been invited to a wedding, that was nice. The wedding has already taken place, because, here they just go to the courthouse and take out a license and then they are married. The girl is an acquaintance of mine, and as a matter of fact, somewhat related to me. She is now married to a Smalander that has been here five or six years and in that time, he has forgotten Swedish, but overall he appears to be a fine boy. He is 23 years old and she is 18 years old so they have married in the Spring of their youth. I can't with the best will in the world avoid feeling somewhat jealous when I see young people get married and be lucky, but why can't I be the same! How can I get married when I never associate with any women?

Since I bought this land I have had to forsake everything. I can hardly refuse to attend this wedding which is what I would like to do because when I see them happy, I think like this. Why am I not married? Don't I have the same right to be happy as these people? I sit here in my wooden box that I call home, always alone, prepare my own food and make my own bed. If I am sad, I have no one to comfort me, and if I'm happy, no one to be happy with. I have no objection to being married. I have no one to be married to, and if I had someone that I could marry, how can I support a wife?

I can hardly go anywhere without meeting people that I owe money to in all because I was dumb enough to buy land. If I had bought land in a new place were the land values goes up in price, then I would've been wise. I then would get rid of it anytime. I would have to live like a hermit in the desert, but many have gotten rich that way. Here I have to live like a hermit in a habitual society, and that is much worse. The worst of it is that I am not getting married or rich either. I believe a girl should be between 20 and 25 years old when she marries and a boy between the age of 20 and 30 years old. As yet, I am not too old for another two or three years. I don't want to bind myself to anyone for my whole life, but I wish that I was somewhere, where a man could associate with the opposite sex. There is a shortage of women, and it makes it difficult for an "old young man" to meet them. I could go and leave every- thing, but it is not easy to lose 8 or $900 and go out and start over again, also a man has to be patient and wait for better days. It could happen that things will get brighter. Now I have put myself in debt again for new clothes so that I can resemble a human being on Wednesday night.

June 14, 1916

I have just had supper that consisted of blackberries and milk. That is a good supper in the summertime. I am doing the best I can to take up my potatoes. I should get between 50 and 60 sacks. I might have gotten 200 sacks had they not frozen. I also watered them a month too late and now it hardly pays for the work. I will only get one half cent a pound for them in the store. A month ago, I could've gotten $.03 cents. It is so hot that you cannot pick potatoes between 11 and 5 o'clock without getting burned up. When I went out at 5 o'clock to pick potatoes it was 108° in my cabin. Now it is only in the 80s, so at night it is cool. I have so much to do that I can hardly keep up with it all. I have to take up the potatoes and drive them into town (I have gotten an old toothless horse to use just for the feed) I'm going to plow up four acres and plant pumpkins on it, then I have to water the vineyard and the orchard.

I have several buggies to paint and have already painted seven or eight this Spring. Johnson wants me to paint on the new high school in Kingsburg. They are building a new high school that will cost $42,000 for the farmer's sons and daughters to go in and while away the time and be educated so as to avoid all coarse and heavy work in the future.

On Monday, I hung the wallcovering for a family. There was a real house mother that milked the cow, prepared the food, and washed the dishes for seven people and still had time to help me nail cloth over holes in a dilapidated ramshackle house that they were going to live in the summer. She speaks Norwegian and blends into Swedish and the children only speak and understand English. The two oldest girls have just graduated from high school. They dressed up in fine clothes and later one of them played and the other sang at a fine piano that must've cost her father many drops of sweat while her mother prepared supper. When she later did the dishes, she got to hear a little song and music again. This is not to criticize the girls, they are not to blame, for this is the system. The dear children are not to soil their fine hands doing the dishes and preparing food. If such girls as these were to marry a man that could not hire cook it would be a sin for both of them.

June 18, 1916

I sent six sacks of potatoes to a wholesale house with CA Johnson and now I got five of them back. They sold one sack for $1.00 (which I will never get to smell) beside Johnson got a fairly nasty letter from them, among other things it said, "where in the hell did you get them"? The trouble was, the potatoes were too small. Johnson thought I could take them home and pick out the largest ones and sell them to the farmers around here, but potatoes that you can hardly get $1.00 a sack for in Fresno, would be hard to sell for $1.75 a sack around here and in all truthfulness, after they had been in the warm shed for two weeks. I now have the potatoes buried in the ground. There are five sacks of small potatoes that I plan on planting in August and harvesting them in November and December if they don't rot first.

Sunday night September 10, 1916

Yesterday was my 27th birthday, but I did not know that until today. The time goes fast and a man is soon old. My youth, at least the best part, is now gone and I have neither had a good time or made any money, so here a man can see that he should think twice before he does like I have done.

I see now that the potatoes were close to my heart the last time I wrote so now I can say that no more potatoes were planted. I watered 2 acres and had planned to plow them up and plant more potatoes, but then it got so hot during the day that a man could not drive the horses without driving them to death. I then thought that the potatoes would dry up for me in such burning heat before they came up, so I did not plant them. The way the weather is now, it would be fine for growing potatoes, but now it is too late to plant and besides I don't have any left to plant because I let some rot and gave some of them away to feed the pigs. I have a half sack left and that I will eat myself.

I have been with Theissen and worked. I got $2.00 a day and food, when I was with him last. Otherwise the price has been $2.25 and feed yourself. Someone else has fruit to pick here for $4.35 a ton. That is good pay. I would have done better to stay here and pick peaches myself but then FM wants me to help him, and I could not refuse. I wonder how soon it will take my common sense to reason out what first and foremost, is best for me. Maybe never!

We will get about a ton of peaches this year but if Anderson had not let the spiders eat up the blossoms last year we would have about 4 tons. Had I not left and stayed here instead, it could have happened that we would've gotten more raisins than what we will get. While I was gone, the red spiders came and ate up the leaves, and half-grown grapes were burnt up by the sun. (The sun burns here in the summer). It is not like in Sweden, a mild and pleasant sunshine, but what I have written before. If I had been here I could've killed the spiders by dusting the vines. These spiders are about 1/10 the size of a pinhead. When they come on the trees they come in such a mass that it takes them less than a week to eat up all the top leaves. On the other leaves they spin their web so it looks like they are full of dust. If I don't forget, I'm going to take a picture in the morning to show how much damage the spiders can do to the vines in the trees. There was a violent thunderstorm two weeks ago with plenty of rain and that was more than the spiders liked. They all died that night, so the vines are beginning to recover again now since the small pests have been killed off. We now have the nicest weather you can imagine and it has been like this since September 1, just the right temperature. 50° in the morning and 90° during the day. That is the temperature that suits me best now that after the hot summer my blood is as thin as if it was half water. The thermometer is now showing 71° and now I think that it is a little chilly, but not colder than if I put on a coat, then I will be comfortable.

The weather is really delightful! The air is clear and clean and still that hardly a leave moves on my little Aspen that I planted the spring. The frogs can be heard croaking down by the river like a half cut off "gneer-gneer". The full moon is shining clear and smiling from the star strewn deep blue heavens and everything is still and peaceful, that even the worst America hater likes California on a night like this.

I have cleaned my cabin today and now I feel it is quite homey. I thrive here much better than any other place I have been since I came to America. This cabin is my home and I also feel like I am at home. When I come in here I am in my own house and on my own land, even though it is not all paid for, neither the cabin or the land. I think about this farm. Here there is good soil but it must have good care which it has not had. If I could only get a team of horses, then this farm would be worth quite a bit of money in a few years because I would manage it. If I could buy out my cousins and own the farm out right, then it could happen that I too, could be successful in a few years.

Now that I've come to like the place, I might be forced to sell and to sell cheap because the Nelsons want to positively get rid of the farm. they have offered the place (to a Swedish boy that is thinking of buying the land and getting married) for $5700, the price we sold it for two years ago. The farm is, (thanks to the fact that I have lived here this summer) worth much more, but it could happen that Johnson won't buy it anyway. I hope not, but if he wants the farm then there is nothing more for me than to say, "yes and amen" to what the Nelsons decide. One of them has said $700 over $5000 and one of them $800 over $5000. It is terrible how much cackling goes on when there are so many involved in a piece of land. I can if I want, refuse to sell the farm, but if I do, then I will have a falling out with my companions, and then it would be impossible to have the farm with them. The best for me, will be that he does not want the farm, but think about it (maybe to me and to you my friend that reads these lines) that you want to positively go home to Sweden, Mr. Lundquist, your longing for home, judging from the preceding, is fairly strong. Yes, that can happen, but if one will use a little logic, then one would come to under-stand that what shall one do in Sweden when you don't have any more money than to pay for the trip and some clothes, and only just so that you can get back again.

If I sell a farm now, I will get about $400 and if I can hang onto the farm one more year then maybe I can sell and for my part get $2400. That is not impossible at all, because it is now that this farm should be worth money. I am doing my best picking grapes. Maybe it is best that I stop writing for tonight. It is surprising how fast this pen can go once you get started to write. I have now written six sides in a short time.

September 21, 1916

It is now pitch black darkness that is now and again lighted up by a clear greenish lightning and then a little rain falls, and that's a little as far as that goes. This rain is coming at a particularly inconvenient time because there are several trays of dried raisins that have not been stacked up before the rain came. The rain came so fast and unexpected that nothing could be done before the rain came over us. I have not been able to get anyone to come and help me pick my grapes but today a couple of farmers came and helped me pick them. If they had known that we were going to get rain so fast then they most likely would have stayed home and rolled together their 7000 trays instead, because if we don't get any sunshine it could happen that the raisins that laid in the rain will rot. I can roll together some of my trays but the most of them are laying out without a cover.

October 23, 1916

The sun is setting in the West and the sky is clear. It is a still and peaceful evening in nature. The temperature is about 80° but that is not sufficient to dry raisins outside.

Since I last wrote in this book we have had much rain and cold so that most of the raisins have been spoiled. About 50% have been sold to the wineries and there you only get $12 for a ton. I saw in the newspaper last week that the wineries bought 25,000 tons of half dried raisins. 15% will dry that have been rained on and the ones that were cold and dark and moldy and ugly in many ways. For them you get only half price, or $.02 a pound. 20% will be good and 35% will sell for $.04 and $.05 a pound. From our grapes we have delivered to the winery, 253 trays. Had they been dry, we would have gotten between $70 and $90, but we got only $18 for them. I have 250 more trays that might go to making wine, but if I can get them dry, I will get $40 a ton for them, or $.02 a pound.

It looks like I will lose the farm in the Fall. We have to come up with $1300 in the Fall, and the income from the farm will be about $300. Where can a man get the other thousand? $1300 is payment on the mortgage. If we could only borrow $3500 then everything would go good with the farm as security. There is a lot of money in the land now, so it should be possible to get a loan now but before this, it was not possible to get more than $1500 on a farm like this.

I am going out this week and hunt up some money. If I ask my friends for advice they will tell me to leave the farm and let my cousins wrestle with that themselves, but if I leave the farm now, I will lose about $800, as much as I own.

October 25, 1916

Today I drove by a place where they are digging sweet potatoes. They are a type of potato that only grows in a hot climate. They are planted in the ground and from them a mess of plants come up, which are then planted like parsnips and roots. They grow new tops and the roots press down on the ground and develop nodules almost the same as other potatoes. I found the biggest potato I have ever seen in my whole life. I took it home and it weighed 9 pounds.

November 15, 1916

It has been quite cold these last few days, so cold there has not been any equal in many years.

Yesterday morning the thermometer read 28° inside my cabin, when we got up and outside it was 20° cold. It has never been that cold since I have been here, and it is not very often that one feels that here.

The election is now over. It has been an enormous fight between the different parties and no one more to blame than Wilson from the opposing parties, but how it is, he has more friends than the other parties, otherwise he would not have been reelected because he was elected by very small majority. The two biggest are, the Republicans and the Democrats, and they have two small parties, the

Socialists and the Prohibition party. The last named have forbidden the drinking of intoxicating drink on the top of their program. Each and every socialist knows what that is, or has given out leaflets in which he, in simple and clear language, explains the situation. These leaflets have been printed in masses of 3 or 4 million copies and sent out over the country. Here is something that was said in one of them: "wheat is now higher in price than it has been since the Civil War. More weight has been sold to the warmongers than has been produced and there is a further increase in shipping prices. If I were president, neither food nor ammunitions would be allowed to leave the country as long as there were hungry people in the United States".

Either Hughes or Wilson will be elected and it will be the same whichever one it is, because they both represent the capitalist, also the old system will continue, namely, snatch the bread from the mouth of the American people and send it to Europe, even ammunition so as together big piles of money that will be owned by a few persons. That was a part of what Alan L Benson has to say about the situation, and if one will change his thinking in some small degree, it will come to the same results and find out that he is right.

November 16, 1916

I am picking my second crop of grapes the best I can. I should get three or four times than $10 a ton. My affairs are about the same as before, but I think that there will be some changes in the matter soon. I was down and talked to Eklund the other day and appealed to his humanity and got him so far as to promise to wait with the $500 that he should have had as payment one more year, but the promissory note and interest on the capital must be paid.

My companions want to sell at any price, just so that they can get rid of the farm. They have offered the farm to Eklund for $6000. If he would pay that much, then all of the debts could be paid. I would lose all that I put into the farm, but they would get a few hundred altogether, whereas I would lose $700 that I put in money and work. Yes, no matter how you turn, you always have a part of your body behind you, and when it rains pudding, the poor have no spoon. I have seen the truth in that this fall. Had I done as I first planned, plant the potatoes in the summer, I could have sold them for $2.50 or $3.00 a sack. That is the price on them now, but "foremost good advice" led me to believe that if I planted them that time of the year, they would dry up and I would get nothing. There was no risk! When I took up the potatoes in June, there were a few left in the ground and they had neither dried up or rotted. In the fall when we get some rain, they started to grow again and now there are more than I can eat up this winter. How many more would there be if they had been allowed to start growing in August?

November 30, 1916, Thanksgiving day

Yes, I should be thankful on this day that I have been able to keep my health, for that is all I have left. The other went with "David's hens under the ice". My cousins help me with this place when I had $200 that I with great pain, earned and saved (and later I have put into the farm between 4 and $500) and now they don't want anything to do with me.

The other day I was down and talk to Eklund and he promised that for my sake he would wait with the final payment one year, and be satisfied with being paid just the interest for one year, about $600 altogether. My part of the raisins is worth $100, and if I could have raised $200 I would've been able to hold on to the farm. It would've been their responsibility to pay this money because all this time I had $200 more in the farm than Knut Anderson and the Nelsons. At the start they asked $5500 and then deducted $250 and that was to go to an American, as commission for making the deal. When I saw that they wanted to sell a farm at any price, I then told them if I got the raisins, the deal could go through. Had I resisted and gone against the deal, I could've held onto the farm-- could happen-- but when my relatives don't want to help you, then no one else will either. Also, I have now given up on this uneven fight.

The farm cost us $6417. We sold it for $6000. From this I lose $700 and the others lose $517 that will be divided between five people, also you can see that I am the scapegoat in this affair, they cannot see that. They just whine over how much they have lost because they helped me out. I can look anyone in the face and say that if Knut did not exist, they would not have helped me with my farm. The farm is now in good shape and it looks like there will be a good harvest next year. Now I am forced to give it all away to a couple of Americans that are so ignorant that after straining, one of them figured out how to hold a pen and figured what such a thing is used for, and after dipping into the inkwell several times, managed to get his signature down which consisted of streaks, scrawls and crooked lines and looked like everything except the signature. After relating the above occurrences, I wonder if anyone can judge me for hardening in my heart, seized with sorrow and grief as I am, and take my reasons and drive them into the place where I can get the best price for them. The Associated Raisin Company can vouch for that and take the money and put it in safekeeping and let my creditors pester me for what I owe them. This I will do if I get a chance, and you my daybook are the only one that knows my plan, because you can keep a secret provided no one steals it from me.

December 13, 1916

I have now taken in my raisins. I took them first to Guggenheim Company but could not leave them there because the man that buys them was not there. If he had been there, I might have gotten five and half cents a pound for them. I had no other choice but to take them to the Associated Warehouse and there I got only 3 1/2 cents a pound cash, and later, when they are sold one cent and maybe more of the profit. The worst of all is that I have had to take back eight boxes. Now L is going to take them into Kingsburg and see if they will take them there and if they don't then I will lose $30 or $35 more dollars on the deal, but what is the difference, when I'm used to losing? Now the question is if L's son-in-law is going to buy the land and pay $500 cash and $500 in the Spring. To my knowledge he has no money, so his brother-in-law and my cousin will have to lay out the money. Oh yes, now they have the money, but when it was a question of helping me, they had none!

Christmas Eve 1916

It looks like it will be the craziest Christmas I have ever experienced. It has been rainy and nasty, yesterday and today, you can only lay inside. I am living together with a couple old bachelor's, one is

45 years old and the other is 60 years old.

Today we" dipped in the pot" and now I am doing my best to cook porridge, while Hilding is getting milk and Sven is out watering and feeding the horses.

Christmas in the past I was always with some of my relatives and I thought that this year Lofgren's would invite me, but that did not happen. The first Christmas I was here I spent with my oldest cousin and he paired me up with a girl so that was a nice Christmas Eve, as nice as any at home in Sweden, but not in the same style. This is the seventh Christmas I'm away from home together with egotistical and self-centered people. So far, hope has not died, and I hope that next Christmas I will celebrate at home with my mother and siblings and there you can celebrate Christmas with vigor. Here in this land, it becomes a poor imitation no matter how hard you try to make it so, it is not like Sweden.

It is now dusk the rains have stopped for a while. Hilding has come home and is stirring in the pot and is mad because Sven has forgotten to salt the porridge. I have now salted the porridge in the good old Swedish custom, I will put in a bean (I don't have an almond).

Maybe I will write more in the morning.

December 30, 1916

I did not get a chance to write anything Christmas day because one of my friends bought a new Ford and wanted me to take a ride with him to visit some other boys. A couple of them had bought themselves some Christmas joy in fluid form and had partaken in the same, so they felt pretty good and had a good time in their surroundings. One of them had been out and got into a fight, so his nose was all bloodied and swollen.

Concerning an almond or bean in the Christmas porridge, the other guys did not want to know anything about that. They are set in their bachelorhood that they are afraid of the almond's (beans) magical powers, if one of them were to get it. I put a bean in the porridge bowl anyway, but Sven saw it, so he took a tablespoon and pushed it aside. However it was, the bean stuck to the spoon, and later when we ate, I happened to get that spoon, so the bean was mine. The sun is starting to shine so now I'm going to go and do some painting.

January 5, 1917

I have just gotten the money for my raisins, as soon as I got the money in the bank, I went directly and sent it to the post office and sent it to Sweden, because I thought that if my creditors here knew that I have money they will do what they can to collect. I have a debt of over $150 in Kingsburg and only got $86.91, so that was more than half of what I owe.

If I ever get any money in a mass, I will pay my debts, including interest, but I will not take my last cent and pay bills that I would not have had except for the farm. Since my debts go with the farm and are connected, when I was forced to leave the farm, so should I have my own free will leave the debts that the farm incurred.

"Dipped in the pot--"dopp i panna" is a custom in

Sweden of dipping bread in the liquid after cooking the Christmas ham. Some people like this very much.

I sent 400 crowns (kroner) to my brother in Sweden that he can borrow through this and more that I plan to send, if he needs it, and if I can get a hold of more and invest in his engineering company. Later when I come home then this money will be nice to have if I want to return here. If he cannot repay me does not bother me in the least but that $813 that I lost on the farm bothers me to no end.

It is foggy and cold in the air today, I should go out and paint today, but since the weather is not suitable, I will stay inside by the stove and feel good.

January 18, 1917 Porterville

This place is about 57 miles south of Kingsburg. I came here to work in a magnesium mine and have been here two days but right now there is not much to do so I am planning on going back to Kingsburg in the afternoon. I could get work with an Italian and work nights for $2.50 for eight hours but then it cost $2.50 a week for room and $.25 a meal for the food. It is 4 miles from here up and down steep hills to the mine so with one thing and another I don't like it here at all. 5 o'clock I will be ready to go back to Kingsburg. Maybe I will write more about this later but now I have no ambition to write. It is as cold as the devil in this room.

January 19, 1917

I am now back in Kingsburg again. I got here about 9:30 and as soon as I stuck my nose in the door, I was informed that the wallpaper I hung in the kitchen a few days before I went to Porterville had fallen down. The incident spread like wildfire around here. I was up there and tore the paper down and planned on hanging new paper, but now they wanted painted instead, so I am painting there now. I will get three dollars for the job, the paint cost $2.65, so I will get $.35 for my work. I did this so there would not be any moaning or ill feelings. I have hung many rolls of paper around here on both plaster and canvas and none has ever come down before.

It was too bad that I did not have a roll of film with me when I was up at the mine. Mines are the right name, for there are about 500 holes in the hills. There are two companies that own them.

January 20, 1917

I was interrupted last night and will soon continue. These companies contract out the work to anyone that can find a place where magnesite can be found. A man can then borrow tools from the company and earn from $3.25- 4.50 a ton for the magnesite he digs up. There were 11 Swedes that had a contract. They could earn between $4 and $5 a day. I tried to get a job with them, but they did not need any more men than they had, and they had four and five men that they paid only $3.00 a day.

Newspaper editor, counselor and a member of the Swedish Parliament, Mr. Enderstedt was on a tour and visited Kingsburg. He was here on Wednesday night. A meeting was scheduled for 7:30 at the high school. I thought that if I was to get a good seat I had better get there early, so I was there at a 6:45, but there already was about 1000 people waiting outside. When you finally got inside it was jampacked with about 800 people that Mr. Enderstedt had to have a second lecture so that all could see and hear how Sweden is thriving just now. He showed about 50 slides from Sweden's different provinces and explained each slide. The lecture was good and also the slides. The hall was unsuitable because those in the front could hear and see good. Those that stood in the middle blocked the view for all that sat in the back, and then there were some boys that were noisy so that Enderstedt had to tell them to be quiet several times for he wanted silence. At the end Pastor Halen threatened to throw them out and then it was quiet for a while. The rude boys, for lack of judgment, could not respect any other land except America, and therefore tried to disrupt the lecture. If it had been a question of casting them out, I would with great relish have gladly helped. I went to both lectures, and at the second there were places to sit because it was not as many people. Naturally much is changed in Sweden since I left there seven years ago and if I live and have my health, I will return before the end of 1917. The first year I was here I thought that when I had 10,000 crowns I would go home, but now I think that when I have enough for the fare and a little more, I will go home otherwise I may never get there.

February 18, 1917

I have plenty of work for a time now and plenty more on hand, both for myself with Sam Anderson a painter in Kingsburg. We are now working in a church in Parlier. It is a big church and cost $14,000. I like the work very much. The boss is good to work for, and you can work as fast as you want so there is a big difference between him and

Johnson.

I have not had any new Sunday clothing a long time, so I have to sit home on Sundays. All the money I got went to the farm, but now that I am solvent, I can keep the money I earn. I have sent to Sears Roebuck in Seattle Washington for a new suit. There you can buy clothes 30% cheaper than here.

Now I should have potatoes and onions to sell, for now they are worth money. When I planted onions in the spring, onion sets cost $.125 a pound. I planted 6 pounds and got 90 and sold them for $.015 so the profit was not so great. Now the onions cost $.15 a pound and if I could have kept the farm, I may be would have had 5000 pounds of onions to sell in a month from now. Potatoes now cost five dollars a sack, and now I have to buy them instead of selling them. But I won't cry, maybe luck will kick me in the rear some time to begin with, I now have plenty of work in my trade and work every day. I have tried to lease a few acres of marshland that has been drained but have not been able to get it as yet. It could happen that I could get a piece that is planted in wheat, and that will be harvested in June. I have half a promise that I can lease this land, so it could happen that I will plant potatoes again.

March 9, 1917

There was a real estate salesman here Wednesday night who wanted to sell lots in Richmond, a town that lies outside of San Francisco. There was a big farm they there in 1900, and just a few inhabitants. In 1906 there were 6,000, and in 1915 there were 32,000 inhabitants and 32 factories, so a man can see that it is a town that is growing and will grow more yet.

I bought a lot and put down $10, and after I see the lot and if want to keep it, I will pay $15 more and then five dollars a month until it is paid. The price is $800. Last year a lot cost $425 so in a year my lot can be worth from $900 to $2000 and maybe more, anyway, the agent is going to take me there and show me the town and all that is worth seeing, and all expenses on the trip. If I were to go on the train the trip would cost $12.50 so the $10 is not thrown away if I don't want the lot.

I will most likely go to Richmond in a month and take my knapsack with and if I find work, stay there and then be able to keep the lot. I don't think I would lose it like I did the farm. It should not be too hard to scrape five dollars a month to pay for it. I would not have to pay interest on the capital and no taxes until lot is paid for, and last but best of all I would not have it together with anyone else I would have it alone. The only thing that bothers me is that it could hinder me from going home to Sweden for Christmas because if I keep the lot I will have to pay $60 a year and that would be hard to do without if I go to Sweden. Later, if I want to stay in Sweden, it might be hard to sell the lot. However strong my longing for home is, maybe it is dumb to travel to Sweden as long as the war continues.

March 25, 1917

When I came to Kingsburg seven years ago almost 10% of the farmers had cars. The others had carriages and buggies drawn by horses, now you see mostly cars on the road. 80% driven are "stink tanks" and half of them are from Henry Ford's factory. They are strong and cheap machines. They now cost $415 and you can get one for $200 down and pay off the rest in six months. Automobiles can be found here from $300-$2900, and maybe some are cheaper and some more expensive, but as I said, half of the machines in the country are Ford's.

April 16, 1917

I was in Richmond and saw my lot but did not like it as much as I thought I would. I could not go in and see the factories because of the war with Germany and I could not find any work either. The agent and I left here Saturday night in a Chevrolet car and came to Oakland in the morning, rented a room and slept for a few hours. Later we drove to Richmond to see what it looked like. I thought it looked good and would keep it and was dumb enough to give the agent a check for $15 on the remainder. Once you put your name on such a paper you are stuck if you don't have money in the bank, then it is best to put it in so I must give up $15.

I was supposed to make the first five-dollar payment yesterday, but I think it is best that I stopped now and not get mired in because it could happen that you would have to hold onto such a lot for 10 years before you could sell it and get your money back. So the $25 I laid out can go to the cost of the trip and then get out while the getting is good. When we rode home I drove for 100 miles or so. That was fun! I drove as fast as 36 miles an hour. As I mentioned before, I have steady work and $3.50 a day but if I go east I can get $4-5.00 a day. I had a letter the other day from a boy. He says there's plenty of work in Rockford and he wants me to come and maybe I will.

May 27, 1917

I am sitting in Kingsburg. It has been unusually cool and nice the whole spring, almost cold, but today it is warm. I am still working for "Uncle Sam". I have become almost indispensable to him. He has a strong belief in me. He thinks there is nothing in the painting trade that I cannot do. Two or three weeks ago we painted a fine house in Kingsburg where the kitchen and bathroom were to be marbleized, so Sam asked me if I knew how to do that kind of work. I told him that I was very interested in that kind of work. I have seen how it is done, and it is not hard to do. White paint is brushed on the wall and a piece of charcoal is used to make squiggly lines and flourishes. They are then stroked over with the brush. It is a sin to say that it looks like marble, but I was interested in doing it right and had seen it done in San Francisco and other towns. Instead of using charcoal I used gray paint and painted out the figures and when the paint set up enough, I blended together the gray paint with the white. From a distance and subdued light, it looks like genuine marble. When Sam saw it, he was so happy that he drove to Kingsburg and bought me tobacco and cigarette paper. When the people that own the house came and saw it, the woman said that she believed that we could do magic. I have since marbleized another bathroom and that one turned out better than the first one. It turned out so good that people came and saw it and gave me admiring glances and they think that I am a real professor in marbleizing. Now I will marbleize wherever I go, and I think that I will be able to do it better yet.

Sam is so delighted and brags about me that I feel uncomfortable. I do all of the finest work. If I said to him that I would quit unless I was better paid than I would get more money, but I am not one to take advantage. The others don't get more than $3.50 a day and that would be good enough for me too.

If I stay in Kingsburg I will have to pay my debts and as long as I have steady work, it is best to stay. I know from experience that you cannot save if you rove about. So most likely I will move down to Kingsburg and stay the summer and pay my small debts and some on the big ones. If I, through some sort of speculation could earn extra money, then I would pay off all of my debts, but if I pay them by working then they may never be paid in full.

June 6, 1917

Yesterday was military registration day in the country. The president has issued an order that all able-bodied men between the ages of 21 and 31 years of age are to report to different places and answer 12 questions. I gathered up my courage and went up to Canal Street School and presented myself before Pontius Pilate that had manifested himself in the form and an old polite and obliging lady. I sat on a stool and she had a card that was full of questions. She then wrote down my answers. The last question was if I had any objections about serving in the military, but since I did not apply for citizenship, and did not have to answer that question, they could not take me because I am a citizen of Sweden. I have never intended to be a citizen because I have never liked it well enough to put my roots down here. It is not through neglect that I am not a citizen of the United States.

In taking out your first papers to become a citizen of the United States, you first have to renounce your loyalty to all European kings and monarchs and most of all your loyalty to King Gustav V of Sweden, and that I do not want to do because Gustaf V is a man that knows what he wants. That he has shown ever since he has been Sweden's king, as a man cages himself to here, the hair will rise on everyman that will use his brain for what it was made for, namely to think with.

First send out ammunition, weapons and food to the belligerent as long as they have money to buy with. When their money runs out you loan them more, then in spite of this they can't get the Germans to bend, Uncle Sam starts to worry that he won't get his money back unless he helps to beat the Germans. So, you simply declare war. Of all the senators and congressmen there are only six or seven that have enough sense to vote against the war. The others voted for it. People put flags in their cars to show that they are patriotic. Think how unfair it is of them that they have decided that we will have a war, not one of them would have to go. They are all too old. The government has requested a loan of $2 billion dollars. That amounts to $20 from each individual across the country. They have alone in Kingsburg requested $40,000 from the farmers. One can wonder if the capitalists have loaned out all their money to the allies?

I wonder, if you press the working class and all the other countries, will they ever cast off their military yoke and stop going out and murdering each other so that one or the other monarch should get a little honor and the cold, calculating money and so men should get a few more possessions?

June 17, 1917

Now we have sun and summer. When I was in Sweden I thought of summer with a longing and burning emotion. Here I think of summer as an experienced person, that one is doomed to be cast in the burning oven. It was 106°F yesterday. The wind was hot and the air was sultry. When I came home last night I felt the coffee pot and it was hot. I asked if they just drank coffee and they told me that the pot was not heated since in the morning. It is hot now I said. Holberg then said that I should feel other things and I would know that it is hot, and so it was. Everything I touched was so hot it burned. I know that it was hot before, and the fact is, that it was that hot last night.

July 15, 1917

It is Sunday 20 minutes before 6:00. I am sitting at the hot table and the sweat is dripping off of me. It is 107° in the shade. Last week it was up to 109° almost every day. It happens that the temperature rises to 120°, but if the air is clear it does not feel as painful as it does now because it is cloudy and sultry and some of the people can hardly breathe. It has been sultry the whole week but when you work you do not feel it as much as when you are resting. The air swarms with flies during the day and mosquitoes at night so if you go out to enjoy nature you are never alone. I took a bath in a canal and to get there I had to walk a mile in loose damp burning hot sand. The water was 3 feet deep hot and muddy. For someone that is used to bathing in crystal clear lakes of Smaland, I get very little satisfaction from that bath but it was somewhat cooling.

Yes, here it is hot, but I have not heard of anyone dying from the heat like on the East Coast. There is a farmer here by the name of Bowman. He was in Imperial Valley. He said it was so hot there that when you are going to milk a cow you had to jump into a canal with your clothes on to cool yourself off and if you had another cow to milk, you had to jump in again. That I wouldn't have believed when I was home in Sweden, that is to say, I did not believe people would want to live in such a climate but now I do. I don't want to live here, but the circumstances are that it is wisest for me to stay and tolerate, now the torture is half gone, and in two months there will be tolerable weather again, so all things have their ending.

We have plenty of work-- so much now that I don't think we will get it done in time. It is now four months since we started them and they are not finished yet. If I wanted to quit now I think it would be hard for me to get out all my money (I have $250 coming) because the boss naturally does not want to let me go. It could happen that I would have to sue him, and that could drag out for a long time. If I go somewhere else I might not get work and if I did, I might not like it. I have a good place here, $4.00 a day for nine hours work, so if I stay here until Fall I will have traveling money to Sweden, and if the war is over I will go, otherwise I will not.

I have named several circumstances where I have been unaccustomed to this country, but for those that are born and raised here it is fine to stay here. If I ever leave here in earnest, I will have to be crazy before I steer my course back here again.

July 19, 1917

As I wrote before all men between the ages of 21 and 31 are registered for the draft, then came the lottery, out of 1,400,000 the figure is that half will be invalids for life, fish food or worm food for the French worms that I have heard are especially ugly. I was one of the lucky ones in the first drawing, but many were rejected, so another lottery was held and in that one I was one that was drawn. On Friday I will stand muster, but as luck will have it, I did not take out my first papers. It is against the law to take me. The foreign-born people that have taken out their first papers have shown that they want to be citizens of the United States are taken before native borns, because it will give them the opportunity to show that they are serious about renouncing their allegiance to their homeland. A senator has just put in the bill that if anyone that is not a citizen that is discharged will have a choice of taking out their citizen papers or be sent home to their respective countries, if that country is an ally of the United States. That motion will most likely pass with a full majority. I heard the other night that people like me, will go in the Army or leave the country for Sweden inside of 60 days after being drafted. If that is true, my choice will be between Sweden or a French trench. Maybe 10 years earlier, I would've chosen a trench, but since my brain has had a chance to develop I have come to the conclusion that there is no honor to go out and murder your fellow man. If that was an honor, then I think that a man would be better off with a little less honor and a little more sense.

When one reads this, they may think I am a coward but that I am not. I would risk my life if it is a question of saving other lives, but it is against my principles to go out and murder my fellow men, even if I am ordered to do so. Also in me, they will get an ugly fish to scale when I come to Fresno.

August 26, 1917

Now I have been weighed on a scale and found out that I am 149 pounds naked. Johnson and I went up to Fresno on Friday. The physical exams took place on the fifth floor of the courthouse. First, we went to the county clerk's office, where I should have told him that I did not take out my first papers, and I would not have to go any further. I thought that if no one asks me I would just go with the crowd, because I wanted to see how the exam was done. I also figured that if I have to lose time and money for my work, then they can give me a free physical exam.

There we went to a large room that looked like a courtroom and sat there until our names were called out. They took 10 people at a time. I was not called in the first or second calling, so I went out and had breakfast. When we came back, Johnson's name had already been called, so he had to wait until 1 p.m. I was in the fourth group called. We then had to show our orders that we had gotten from Washington DC. Then they gave me a paper with that we went into another room. A dentist came and put a tongue depressor in our mouth to see how many teeth we had. I had 28 and all in good shape, that was then written down on the paper they gave us, then I went to a doctor that examine my eyes ears and nose and then I was alone in that room. We then went into another room that was divided into cubicles. We went to a cubicle and took off their clothes, and then went to a scale to be weighed and measured. I was 69 inches long and my chest measured 38 inches. From there we went to the table where we were asked if we were healthy and had we ever been in a hospital or madhouse. Later we went to a doctor that examined our mouth ears nose lungs heart stomach and testicles, and also took our temperature. When he came to my two blown off fingers, he called over another doctor and asked him if he should reject me, but the other doctor said that I was too nice a man to be rejected so then I was accepted.

I then went to a man and gave him my paper that was written on it "normal okay all over". I then got a card that said I was accepted. I then went and put on my clothes. When I went out I showed this card to a corporal that stood by the door. He asked me if I had any objections to being drafted or if I wanted to be released. I then told him that I had not taken up my first papers yet. He then became a little angry and asked why went through the physical. I told him that it was up to them to ask me what kind of cuckoo I was before they examined me. I then went to the county clerk's office and turned in my exemption, there I got abuse again because I let them examine me so I answered them the same as before.

They wrote on the paper that I was a foreigner (not German) that has not taken out his first papers. He then told me that I should go and buy a form 119. What do I need that for? That is a paper that says you swear that you have not taken out your first papers. Where can I get one of these papers? You can get that paper here in town and then you have to fill it out yourself, otherwise, if you don't get it you will be taken to the front lines. That was not much of an answer but I thought that I would go into town and have a beer and mull it over. I asked everyone that I met if they could tell me where to get a form 119. No one knew even what it was. I then got back to the courthouse and asked a different girl where I could get that form to release me. She took pity on me and wrote down the address on a piece of paper. So, when everything came full circle this form could be bought in the bookstore for $.10. Later I went to a lawyer in the courthouse and he filled in the form 119. How old I was when I came to America and that I had not taken out my first papers. I then had to hold my hat in my left hand and raise my right hand and swear to the fact that everything I told him was the truth, then I was released. If I had taken out my first papers as soon as I came here, (Which you can do) there would have been schemes in the air for not letting go. I should write more, but I'm tired of writing.

September 17, 1917

"Today red, in the morning dead"

I planned on writing the other night and did so, but did not get any further because the lamp went out-- somehow or other water gets into the kerosene tank. Now it is Sunday, the 9th of September, my birthday. As usual we went to work Tuesday morning. When we got there Sam noticed that he forgot to bring his lunch but it did not matter because he had to go to Fresno and get some varnish anyway. I wrote down a list of materials that he should buy. I included three bottles of wine for myself (I like to have a glass of wine once in a while. It is a good buffer against the paint smell and the climate). Sam also likes to have a drink once in a while but the worst of it is that he never knows when he has had enough. Then he wants whiskey and that is seven times worse than wine or beer.

So Sam went and he was supposed to be back by noon but did not show up that night either so I went home. The next day I waited for him until 8 o'clock and then I walked to the job. When I got there, I learned that Sam was dead. He had rolled over his Ford and was pinned so that the blood vein in his head had broken and caused a cerebral hemorrhage so that he died of later that day.

It was a shocking surprise for me, especially due to the fact that he owes me $350 on the house I am working on now. Sam has already been paid $300 and the job is worth $400, and the rest cannot be done for $150. So how it goes I can be thankful that I still have my life. It was risky to ride with him many times. He came within a hairs breathe many times close to rolling over. Two days after the accident I sent the man that owns the house that we are painting to Selma for varnish and my wine. The varnish was there, but the basket where the wine was supposed to be was empty. At first I thought it he had forgotten to buy the wine. I heard later that they found four bottles of whiskey in his machine. I figured that it was my three bottles of wine and a bottle of whiskey that he had bought for himself, but what happened to it? Those that found it most likely drank it up and said that there was booze in the car. When his wife and three small children hear this, their pain and sorrow will be doubly hard to bear especially since they did not know that he drinks. He has been careful to keep that awful secret from his family.

September 18, 1917

A little time has now gone by since Uncle Sam's death and now it is time to think about the other part namely money. Once in a while I get $10, $20,

$40 and up to $60 at a time from Sam on occasion, and each time I wrote the amount down in my book. When we worked eight hours a day I got $3.50 a day and when we worked nine hours I got $4.00 a day. I had been after him many times to settle our account but he always managed to slip away like an eel. In the afternoon, I went to Fresno to review the work that was done. I then went to Sam and told him I wanted a definite time when I would get my money for the work that is finished. I told him that he could not pick up many workers that are as loyal to him as I had been and he should be just as loyal to me, and that he agreed to, and said that I would get my money in 14 days. I then I then told him that I would not do any more work after 6 September if I did not get my money. I did not have to go on strike, Sam died on the fourth.

The biggest job we have is for a blind Armenian by the name of Serian. Sam Anderson had a price of $450 for that job. He had already been paid $300 on the job and it cannot be finished for what is left. I have $160 coming on that job and I believed Sam when he said that he did not get paid any money in advance.

There is a strong law in California that protects the worker a lawyer told me yesterday. He said that a worker can get his money from the homeowner when the work is finished within 90 days but if you wait longer you will get nothing. I have gone to the homeowners and told them how much money I had coming and that I wanted my money before Friday otherwise I would have to turn it over to my lawyer. They then said that the law could not be so wrong as to make them pay twice. I said the law is right if it is not wrong and is the same for everyone. Now I am going to talk to the lawyer and see if they are compelled to pay me. Anyway, they have promised to pay me.

By rights Mrs. Anderson should pay but she has no money and did not know anything about Sam's business affairs, so I would not want to be hard on her if I don't have to. No matter how you look at the situation it is wrong. If I should lose, if the homeowner has to pay twice or if the widow with three small children should pay debts she did not know about until now-- all are wrong.

The only thing a man in the right can demand is an accounting in order to obtain justice. I say that the biggest injustice is whether I should lose the money that I have worked long and hard for or not. If there are any plans in the air for me to get my money I will do so, even if I'm forced to give half of it to lawyers. Johnson the painter has offered me five dollars a day to work for him. I will think it over.

October 17, 1917

It is hot as the devil and if everything goes as I want, I will soon leave here. If I can get my money, I will travel to Sweden to be home for Christmas. I don't care about the expense or anything else. My longing for Sweden is just as strong as it was to come here eight years ago. That time my will was strong and I hope it is just as strong this time.

I am longing to see my mother and my siblings. I want to inhale Swedish air and want to feel Swedish soil under my feet. I want to see snow and rim frost once again on the birch trees back home. I want to hear the organs murmuring sounds in my birth parish church. I can see all of this in my mind. I WANT TO GO HOME. Anyone that is far from home knows what kind of longing that is.

I am soon finished with a big house that we are painting for the Armenian. He has promised to pay me for my work, but only the work done since Sam died. That is only $100. Before Sam died I had $160 coming. He is going to ask a lawyer if he has to pay that. The lawyer that I talked to said that I can get my money 30 days after the notice of completion is filed, but I cannot get my money until the work is done. I can then positively draw out my money, but it could possibly take as much is six months before I get paid. It could be that the lawyer the Armenian talked to (to make money) said that he does not have to pay me. In that case I will have to sue the Armenian and he would undoubtedly lose. It could happen that he would have to pay $1000 instead of $160 and then I would have to wait a long time for my money, that would hurt both of us. It would be best if he pays me. We would avoid a lot of trouble and maybe I could go home for Christmas. I have $54 coming from Bernhard Nelson. I am sure to get my money from him and I have $67.50 coming from A.P. Carlson. If he doesn't pay soon I will have to pester him. I have been easy-going before but I now I have to be hard handed or else it can go for me like it did for my father. Everything went down the drain for him because he did not stand up for his rights enough of the time. I'm going to show these guys that they are not dealing with a weakling.

November 1, 1917

I have now come so far that I can say like "Frithoff" one more time I want to spend Christmas in the North. I plan to leave here November 8 and be in New York on the steamship Bergenfjord. If nothing unforeseen happens then it will be a reality that I have longed for, for such a long time. It may not be too smart to travel to Sweden now, but I am thinking that if I don't go now, I may never get home again. I have enough money now to take me home and I think that now it is going to happen. I have waited for this time ever since I came here and could have gone home before this if I had not followed "good" advice as much as I did--- this is all previously related. I got $30 from Palm and Bernhard Nelson loaned me $50 that I will pay back. The Armenian paid me for all the work I did since Sam died and $100 of the $160 I had coming while Sam was alive. So I got $219 from him. I thought it best that I take what I could get from the homeowner. If I have pressed a little harder, I might've gotten $50 more.

Most likely there won't be much left of Sam's fortune after the investigators get theirs, but if there is anything left I will get $101 before other any other creditors get theirs. Sam's life was insured for $1500 and if his wife understands and appreciates how loyal I was to her husband, then she would pay me when she gets the insurance money but there is not much hope of that, so that $101, I might never see.

I had about $150 in debts last fall that I was not going to pay, but this summer I have paid about half and will pay the rest when I get my money, but not before. This week I worked for CM Johnson and got $3.75 a day for eight hours. He wants me the whole winter if I want to work and be my own boss, and have all the work I want.

I'm glad that money has not been in control of my good feelings and that I can cast out economic profit and calculating and follow my feelings. Two weeks in Sweden with siblings and my mother will balance out in full all the money I earned during the summer and all I could earn in the winter, so if my unlucky star does not become too obstinate I will spend Christmas at home with my mother this year.

November 7, 1917

I am now ready to leave for Sweden. Johnson the shopkeeper came up today and wanted money so I gave him a note on account that Thorston and Algot signed. When I get my money from Anderson's estate I will pay the note and if I don't get the money then Algot and Thorston will have to pay it, and then I will pay Algot but I will never pay Thorston.

I was up by my cousin Gulbrand. He was ashamed. He cried and wanted me to not be angry with him so I said that I wasn't and to tell the truth, I wasn't. He has not fulfilled his obligation to me, but it would only hurt me to be angry and not Gulbrand.

I owe the lumberyard $10, and Carlson and Sherling $4.50. I hope that these bears don't come and lay their gloves on me tonight before I leave. Yes, here in my daybook one can read my feelings like an open book as they say.

END OF BOOK 5

BOOK 6

RETURN TO SWEDEN

November 9, 1917 San Francisco California

Carlson and Sherling came up to Lindholm's at night while I was there to say goodbye, so I paid them what I owed. Later when I got to the station at 11 o'clock, Carlson was there and stared like a bull and wondered why I did business like that. I said that Palm paid Carlson my money for AP Carlson's and when I get it I will pay but since you cannot rest easy because of $5.40 you will get it now. So I took out my pocketbook and paid him. When he felt the money in his hand he became so glad that he took my hand and wished me a good trip, but Verble from the lumber company I did not see, and if he had come he would not have gotten his money. I am glad that there is enough energy to set aside all my obstacles and drive my will through and go to Sweden.

We left Kingsburg at 11 o'clock and arrived in San Francisco 8 o'clock the day after. There were four of us from Kingsburg. First we went to the Consulate and got our passes with our pictures pasted on them. We looked a little grim on them after sitting all night on the train. We then went to the ticket agent and got my ticket, and then everything was settled. I sent the money order home to my mother for $75 so if I wind up on the ocean bottom she will inherit something from me. I got 270 crowns and 21 ore in exchange. I hope it gets there so I will have it when I get home. You are not allowed to have any letters with you to Sweden. You can then get in trouble.

The post office in San Francisco is a finest I have ever seen. The walls and floor are of marble. I think it cost several million dollars. I think I will go out and visit one of my old bachelor friends that was in the Philippines for three years, and is now laying sick in a hospital in San Francisco. We are going to leave here at 1:40 in the afternoon. I think that we will stop and see the world notorious city of Salt Lake.

I went to the military camp but could not find either Knut or Simon. So now I am sitting in the hotel room waiting for my comrades. We will leave at 1:40 in the afternoon.

I just wonder if they have handy elevators in Sweden like they have here. Whichever floor you are on, you just push a button and the elevator comes. When you step inside and want the 10th floor you just press number 10 and you come to the 10th floor in the hotel, push on B and you come to the basement level and so on.

November 15, 1917

We are now in the big city of New York. We arrived last night and are in the Hotel Cornish Arms. I was out for a while to see the town, but it is so big that you can't see much in a few hours. I'm going out again in the afternoon and see as much as I can.

We left San Francisco Friday the ninth and traveled through California, Nevada, Utah, Wyoming, Colorado, Nebraska, Iowa, Illinois, Indiana, Ohio,

Pennsylvania, Maryland, New Jersey and New York. It was mighty slow riding through Nevada, Utah and Wyoming, just barren land, only sand and weeds. Snow could be seen on the mountain tops all around. We came to the notorious Salt Lake in the middle of the night. We rode on the Southern Pacific to Ogden, Utah and on the Union Pacific Railroad. The climate is about the same as California. We were too far north of the city to see it. When we got to Utah, the land was fertile, thanks to the Mormons that transformed that sand desert into paradise. We arrived in Omaha, Nebraska at midnight and into Iowa early sunrise. That is a fine state, corn and wheat all over, and more. We came to Chicago at night. There was a horse and carriage that took us to the Ohio and Baltimore station, and we rode that train to New York. We stayed in Washington DC one night, so there was not much time to see the capital. We did not see the White House either as time was so short. Between Chicago and New York, the land is much like Sweden, except the houses are more in the old English style. There is a huge difference between the East and the West, concerning appearance-- San Francisco is ahead of New York. San Francisco was raised from the ashes after the earthquake and fire 10 or 12 years ago. It looks like I won't be able to take home any coffee, so I may have to leave it in Halifax, Canada. The rate of exchange here in New York is $.37 to the crown. That is a low rate but if you can't get more than you have to be satisfied with that.

New York City November 18, 1917

We are still in New York. The boat was supposed to leave on the 17th but now won't leave until the 20th. Scandinavian American Line's steamboat, Helig Olaf is to leave then so as to travel together with another boat in case one of them hits a mine or is sunk by a submarine the other one can pick up passengers. We are staying in a hotel and paying $2.00 a day. That is $.75 too much for room and board, but then there is no sense in moving if the boat leaves in two days. I have heard that this is a big city but I did not think it was this big. We have been riding on elevated trains, streetcars, subways and railways and no matter how far you ride there is no end in sight. We rode over the mighty Brooklyn Bridge, Manhattan Bridge and more. Here there are railroads that go in tunnels under the Hudson River in several places. If one wants to see all the worthwhile sights here, it would take a month.

We were down by the boat the other day and had our trunks inspected and marked O.K. Everything that is going on the boat had to be seen by the authorities before it was loaded on the boat. There is a mass of Scandinavians that are going on the boat, most of them between 21 and 31 years old. You have to have a registration card and exemption certificate and a pass from the consulate before you can leave.

One can think that in this country that is "flowing with milk and honey" there would be plenty of food, but such are not the conditions. The hotel manager called and asked for 20 tons of coal. He was told that he can only get two tons. The manager told us that he can only get from 3 to 5 pounds of sugar at a time and real sugar can't be had at all. The sugar we get here is raw, brown and moist. It can happen that the government here will do as they do in Sweden, give out bread and sugar cards.

I don't think I will write anymore until I am rolling

on the blue waves. I'm going to put this book on the bottom of my suitcase because if the authority should see it, they may want to read it before I can travel home. If one can believe what you read in the papers you can't buy rice in Sweden now, and so that I don't have to do without my Christmas rice porridge, I will take home two pounds with me.

November 21, 1917, Bergensfjord

We are somewhere between New York and Halifax Canada. We left New York at 6 o'clock last night and slept on the boat the first night. The last night in New York we went to the Hippodrome, the largest theater in the USA. What we saw was a mild variety show. There were about 200 people in the scene at one time and in order to see everything you would have to have 10 pairs of eyes. I won't try to describe what we saw, because I can't do that. Sometimes it was like the story "Thousand and One Nights". It was all like a shimmer. We saw dancing girls, daredevil acrobats, steamboats, steam engines, marching soldiers, bathing beauties and more. If one wants to see genuine American grandeur in a unique class, then the place to go is the Hippodrome, but for my part I don't think much of it, and when I have seen that kind of show once, then I have had enough.

We went to the dock yesterday morning. It was so full of people that it was like being in purgatory before you showed your pass and had it stamped, then you had to have your tickets stamped. After that you had to get someone see your bags and other travel articles and have them marked with chalk because everything that was going on the boat had to be marked. When that was done, the proper torment began. That was when you had to stand and wait to get through a narrow door. It was so narrow that you were pressed flat as a pancake. If by chance you closed your fist, you would not be able to straighten it out again. I tried several times to put down my bags, but I could not bend over. I could have let go of the handles but if a corner of them had touched the floor, I would not have been able to pick them up again. I tried to hold them in another hand, but that was impossible. You moved ahead inch by inch in the stream. After three hours, I was finally up to the mighty man that then decided if I could go or not. First I came to a man that looked at my pass then there was another that asked me some questions that went like this "where were you born? How old are you? How long have you been here? The last question was like this: "I suppose you took out your first papers?" No! "You should be ashamed that you have been here so long and did not take out your first papers".

I did not think fast enough otherwise I could've answered what is the truth, that I came here to see how it was here and never intended to stay and did not want the first papers if I could have earned enough money to pay my passage home long before now. I answered that a person does not have any obligation to take out any papers, and it is not to help the people from Europe to let them come here. It is because they need workers that can do the heavy work for heartless capitalists that run the country and become richer and more powerful. If a person looks at the bottom of the poor quarter of Brooklyn and New York, you can see things that you would never see in Sweden. I have seen street urchins in Brooklyn freezing, starved and ragged that you would never see in Europe.

It is true that if a person goes to the desert in a new

settlement and lives away his youth by working and sacrificing, he can reach independence in his old age. A few hardheaded people without conscience can become richer quick by speculating and wild gambling, it can also go the other way. Out of six of us boys that lived in Kingsburg one winter, I am the only one that managed to get enough money together for a ticket home. Knut and Simon are in the Army; Carl is in Moline Illinois. Arthur was in a training camp a few days and was let go because he had poor teeth. Walter hired on a sailing vessel and got home that way, and now I am on my way home. It is storming and raining pretty heavy now.

November 22, 1917

I had to stop writing yesterday. They came and set the table. We are laying at anchor outside of Halifax and don't know how long we will stay here. Some people think five days. There is no one that knows what John Bull will decide. We had a very stormy night and there were many that called to Ulrik at sunrise. When I came up on deck it was storming and the waves were billowing so bad that I too almost called out to that Ulrik. I went down to my cabin and slept a while and then I felt good. We got good food on the boat the bread is good. It is like you baked it yourself. Our waiters are nice so one can feel at home here.

We had preachers and singing last night. There were three Norwegian preachers that preached and some played guitar, mandolin and flute. We even had a brass band on board, so music is not missing. When we left New York, there was a guy here that called himself "Varmland's guy". He was in full swing and felt good and sang and hollered so that everybody had a good time with him. Most of them that are going home are young between 21 and 31 years old and Norwegian. There are about 20 Norwegian women in third class, there are not many Swedes, but that is just as well. Norwegians are just as good. That will be all of the writing for a while. Now if I can hide this book so that the stuck-up Englishman doesn't get a hold of it then it will be good.

Yesterday we learned what we have to do if we are torpedoed or hit a mine. If one or the other happens we are to go down to our cabins and put on our life vest and then go up on deck and find a lifeboat. We then pretended that we were in danger and 10 minutes after the whistle sounded everyone was up on the deck with their life belts on. The only thing I'm afraid of is hitting a mine. I don't think we have to be afraid of submarines. It is true that in America the Germans are painted as demons, but I don't think they would sink a boat that they could not profit from.

November 23, 1917

We are in Halifax and we have been here a day and most likely will stay until Saturday night. This is a fine harbor and we are anchored almost in. Next to us is the Danish boat Helig Olaf.

Everything on these boats are inspected. There are also three sailing ships at anchor, one from each of the three Nordic Kingdoms. There are boats from almost all the European countries that the whole world says that the Englishmen have confiscated.

I have heard that the German minister to Argentina with his whole staff is on board and have taken over the whole first-class section. If that is so then we don't have to be afraid of Kaiser Wilhelm. I have met a boy from Eksjo that is on his way home. He left Sweden in August. He says that you can earn good money in Sweden now and the food shortages are not as bad as they believe in America. He said that now that the dollar is worth so little you can earn more money in Sweden than in America and live like a man back home. As we slowly glided into the harbor we passed a large transport boat loaded with soldiers on their way to the front. They waved at us and we waved back. A depression came over me when I thought of the destiny these lively happy youngsters are going to meet.

Most of us here are boys that are going home for fear of being drafted. I'm not going home because I'm afraid of being drafted because I never believed that they would take anyone that does not have their first papers, but who knows what can happen? Maybe all of them will go on strike whether they are citizens or not.

It has stormed and rained the whole night but it is not cold. We are like a big family here. All are polite and courteous. We ate good food and slept good, the bathing is a little hard. We pass the time the best we can, some dance some read or write and others play cards and talk and swear because we have to lay over in Halifax for so long.

Varmland's guy sang on deck this afternoon. A Norwegian and a Dane gave a recitation. I thought of giving them a Swedish recitation also, but I did not feel good. I froze because I did not have my fur coat or galoshes on me, so that will have to wait until another time for me to recite.

November 27, 1917

It is 8 o'clock. We left Halifax at four in the afternoon after having to stay there for five days. We were there two days before they came on board. Later on Sunday, we first had to show our passes. Monday, they inspected all the cabins, knapsacks and trunks that belong to the German minister and his staff. Everything edible found in their trunks was taken away from them. All the trunks were elevated up on deck to be inspected. If they would have taken the time to inspect them all, it would take a whole week. Today was biting cold so that is why the inspector came and said that no inspecting will be done unless we can have peace and quiet. As each one shows their pass they were asked if they had any written material with them. Some said that they did, and it was taken away from them. Had I been dumb enough to say that I had this book, they would've taken it. When they asked me if I had any writing, they got a positive "NO". I then hid my book. Had they found it, it could happen that they would have taken the book and me too. The boat has already begun to rock 'n roll so it looks like a good possibility of being seasick in the near future.

December 1, 1917

The boat is rocking on the blue waves so bad that most of the people have done like the widely known "Petter Jonsson". They have crawled under their blankets. We are now out in the middle of the Atlantic about 500 miles south of Greenland. This boat travels about 335 miles a day and has a speed of 13 to 15 knots an hour (the Lusitania did about 24 to 26 km an hour). I felt a little sick the first two days from Halifax, so I ate very little so that I would not throw up. Some ate as if they had not seen food in two days and when they came to the stairs, they threw everything up. I recommend staying in bed when you become seasick and eat toast and juice, oranges or apples and no solid food.

I was up on deck yesterday and stood in the stern. Sometimes we rode up as high as 15 feet and quickly down again just as far. The waves are from top to top three or 400 feet long and come right at us, so it is up and down hill endlessly.

From what I understand we had a burial on board today. It was a boy from Norway that could not enter the country because of consumption. He has since then laid in the hospital and yesterday he died. His sickness was most likely due to the journeys hardship.

Now it cost $91 to travel from Bergen to New York. That is more than it cost me from Sweden to California eight years ago. It is storming and raining terribly hard now. The boat is rolling and I feel like I have to throw up. The time is 10:20 here in New York 7:20 and in California 4:20 and in Sweden 1:20.

December 3, 1917

Sitting on my bed I am so tired of this trip that I cannot find words strong enough to describe how I feel. We had a powerful storm again last night. I was thrown from one side to the other and could not sleep. Here and there they were lying throwing up. The washbasin and other things fell to the floor with a thud. There is a repulsive stench in this section is below the waterline, and there are no windows that can be opened. Many people have stayed in their beds ever since we left Halifax. If I ever get on land I will never get on this boat again and hope that I never cross the Atlantic again on any other boat either.

December 5, 1917

We are now near Bergen. It is 1:30 and I figure that we will be there by 11:00. Yesterday morning when I had breakfast, the boat rolled so bad that two plates fell off the table and broke. There is a 1-inch-high edge on the table. It is surprising how a man can change. Had there been such heavy rolling when we left Halifax, I would not have been able to eat, even if I was given the whole of Smaland, but now I just hang onto the table and eat with a good appetite. The Harbormaster stopped us last night and examined the captain's papers and then we were allowed to pass.

The storms have quieted down but the waves are still strong. The weather is mild and cloudy we are exchanging our money into crowns here on the boat. We get three crowns for a dollar Norwegian money. They do not have any Swedish money. I am so impatient to get home that I think the time is going at a snail's pace. Down in the cabin some men are lying in their beds smoking sour pipes so all the air is full of terrible smell.

December 7, 1917

Is now a month since my journey started, a whole month!!! We are gliding at full speed between Norway's fjords. Here and there a house is seen on the cliffs with light coming from the windows. They look so inviting and homey. The weather is especially mild and delightful (for example in Halifax it was cold enough to freeze your nose off).

Now it is almost like a pleasure cruise. The boat is going quiet and steady and through the open windows you can hear the steam puffing up through the smoke stacks and it sounds exactly like on a train.

We should have been in Bergen the day before yesterday night at 10 o'clock but did not get there until 6 o'clock last night. When we got so close to the coast but we could not see the cliffs because of the thick fog so we were not able to tell where we were. There was nothing else to do but throw out the anchor and lay still the whole night. It was raining hard in Bergen (a beautiful city) I was so interested in seeing that I did not notice that my fur coat got as wet as a dish rag. Norwegian boys came on board and sold the Norwegian paper "**Tideal Tegn**" for five ore. I counted up to eight cars with new tires on them that waited by the unloading ramp.

December 10

I am now luckily home and fortunate to be home with my mother. We got to Kristiansand at 7 o'clock at night, then stayed there an hour and then continued to Kristiana and got there in the morning and stepped on land. When I came out of the customhouse and saw snow on the ground and sleighs, I thought that I was already in Sweden. Bells jingled and the people walked at an easy pace on the street. They did not have to run like they do in America. The weather was mild and beautiful. We took a streetcar to the railway station. I at once observed the cars were painted a beautiful light blue (not varnished in a hopeless gold brown color like in America) and glided without any noise and rode softer than in America, which made a satisfying impression on me. I thought that everything was so quiet and peaceful and unlike the restless and noisy America.

The train cars in third class were not stuffed sofas like in America, but they were small nice compartments for eight people with a table in each room and a good place to put your travel effects on. Everything was clean and nice and made a good impression. It was not as soft and you could not lounge about as fine as you could on the American plush sofas, but if you want to pay just as much as you do in America, then you can ride in first or second class and that is much finer and comfortable than can be seen in America. I have seen only one class there and it is less than second class in Sweden. The train went with a speed of "la snail" which was all right since they have to fire the engine with half coal and wood in these war times. It is certain that I knew it is beautiful in Scandinavia but that it was so charmingly beautiful, I did not remember. We rode forward down the slope between silver spruces and birches, boulders and snowdrifts where grass showed through here and there, and among all this beauty stood a sturdy built house in the typical Nordic style.

Here and there a few woods jutted inland and when I saw all of this and felt a pleasant error I was almost ready to do, as the Americans do, when they watch a baseball game namely, hop, stamp, whistle and clap their hands and squeal with delight. I then came to remember that I am Swedish and that it is expected to be beautiful here.

Sometimes the train went so slow as a funeral procession. Only one thing was missing and that was the bell like they have on the locomotives in America that sound like a funeral mass.

Just before we reached the Swedish border, Norwegian officials came on the train looking for coffee, rice and weapons and things of that sort, and if they did, they confiscated them. If anyone was bold enough to ask if they would get their things back, they politely answered "Nega muli just write to the toll Commissioner." I think that they confiscated upwards of 20 kg of coffee and rice that the Swedish had with them from America and these high officials will enjoy while they laugh and read the letters from the former owners that are sitting home and drinking brand coffee and eating oatmeal thinking about rice porridge, frowning and looking mad.

I just had 2 cups of good morkjava. I had 11 pounds in my trunk that was not opened until we got to Goteborg and I did not have to pay toll on it. We laid in Goteborg overnight. It cost two crowns to have our trunks moved from one station to another. There is a big difference between a town in Sweden and America. When one comes into, for example, San Francisco, it is full of cars and some cabs and their drivers and chauffeurs name a mess of hotels so that you can get dizzy in the head. Here in Goteborg they meet you on foot and almost whisper when they ask if you want a room. You then ride the apostle horses (on foot) to the hotel. The streets are fairly empty of people. The town looks like it had about 10,000 inhabitants. At first sight, such a town in America would look like a big town.

The room was fine. It had a Kakeugn (a heat device) and electric lights and more. It was not like a room in America. There are all the rooms look cold and naked that you almost freeze even when it is warm. The beds are soft and nice to lay in. The rooms would be homey and fine if they weren't always so cold.

When we came to Falkoping we went into a restaurant and had coffee and cake. You got as much coffee as you wanted, but bread, only as much as your ration card allowed. The coffee cost 25 ore a cup. When we got to Nassjo we had to wait three hours so we went to a café with our knapsacks because to put them in a locker that cost 25 ore a piece but here it was only 10 ore.

At the café, we met the most insolent lady I have ever seen. She did not believe that we had been in America because we did not speak American. There were some young boys drinking coffee and when they were finished she shouted, " up with the money!" And when they did not respond fast enough to her command, she asked what kind of dummies they were that did not have enough sense to pay, so that she did not have to wear out her jawbone arguing with them. We asked her if we could get some food and then she said that it would be better if we went back to America, because there is no food here. I thought that the whole thing was so comical that I could not help but laugh out loud.

Between times we went out into town to see if we could get some food. I said to my companion that if we were in a town as big as this in America you would not have to look long before you saw a sign with "restaurant" printed in big letters. Sometimes we found a café or Konditorie, but they were closed, at last we came to a café and there was a man that told us that it was closed. I asked him if he knew how a man could get some food. He called out to a girl to show us a boarding house that we could not have found by ourselves because there was no sign.

We went in and asked if we could get dinner." Do you have a ration card?" we were asked. When we said yes, we were promised food. The food was set out in the middle of the room on a table. You then went and helped yourself and sat down at a small table nearby and ate. The food was good-- prepared in true Swedish style, and you could eat as much as you wanted. The bread was not at all like they had in Sweden eight years ago. It was coarse and baked in thin cakes and poorly risen, but it tasted good anyway. You could get so much and no more but then you got all the potatoes you wanted. I would have been satisfied with half as much. All of this cost only $1.50. That surprised me when I thought of the inflation in Sweden that is on the border of famine. In America, such a meal would've cost $.50 but it would not have tasted as good.

Luckily, I got in the carriage of H. N. J. It appeared small to me and dark and went so slow that you would think it was pulled by a pair of old oxen, but at last we came to Malmback, and then my journey was finished.

ALBREKT HOME AT MALBACK

It is not possible to buy lamp oil in Sweden, but I am sitting here by a lamp, writing, that is just as good. My brother made it. It burns with carbide and water. The invention is quite simple. The bottom of a bottle is knocked out, hang a bag of carbide in the bottle, mount a gas burner on top of the bottle with plaster so that it is airtight. A glass jar is filled one quarter full of water (which is plentiful in Sweden) and the bottle is placed inside. The burner is then lit. At first the flame is as small as a pea and is dim.

It is the air that was in the bottle that burns that way. The water level in the jar has to be just right so that the bottom of the carbide sack touches the water surface. If the flame is too high you just take out some water if it is too low, just add more water.

December 17, 1917

I was hoping there would be snow on the ground when I got home, instead the ground was bare and slushy like it is usually at Easter. In the morning when I looked out there was snow on the ground and the snowflakes were falling slow and pretty and then I thought that was fine. It seems very strange to sit here in the pleasant warmth of the Kakelugn (heater) and look at the room then for "Jack Frost has painted on the windows". Last night I saw something I have never heard of being seen in California, or as a matter of fact, I have not seen before, namely the Aurora Borealis, Northern lights.

My brother and myself had just been to Malmback and as we neared home we saw streams of light in the north that look like sunrays through the clouds. It then started to flame in the West and became brighter and brighter. At the end, the sky was half covered in a white shimmer and everything like it was on fire. It flamed like the flames in a white-hot fire.

For me, it was a show worth much more than any vaudeville show I have seen in America. It was absolutely beautiful.

We were out cross-country skiing yesterday. It was nice but we were on a small pond so you could not ski with any vigor.

It's surprising how I think that everything is little here at home the trees are small and the roads are narrow and the smallest are the farmer's wagons. I think they look like toys. When I compare the over "face powdered" ladies in America and the Smaland lassies, the advantage falls to the latter, and here it is as it has always been. The young get together and have a good time and don't give a damn what the priest or preacher say and don't need horses nor automobiles in their play, they go together and play and dance and amuse themselves to their hearts content and then later the boys follow each one's girl home.

Fourth day of Christmas 1917

I'm sitting home writing the weather has been splendid the whole Christmas and today is especially beautiful. The rim frost is hanging on the bushes, the sun is shining, the heavens are high and clear, and the air is fresh and pleasant. The temperature is about 32°F. The ground is covered with six or 8 inches of snow that glistens like diamonds in the sun. A man can hardly describe how wonderful this land is. In order to know that, a person has to come here and see for themselves. Here is fine sleigh riding but the snow cover is too thin for cross-country skiing. I was out skiing since I came home, but the ice was not very good.

I went to Christmas Eve. An absolute solemn feeling came over me when I saw the candles burning, saw our old priest in his mass attire, and heard the roar of the old organ. It really isn't old, it is only nine years old, but it is big and fine and when it played, it almost lifts a person off of the pews. I'm almost a little too lazy to describe all of this. I at least want to write that this Christmas was well worth returning home for. Just think how dumb I would have been had I not traveled back home. If I had stayed in Kingsburg, I would have lain there like a swine. Now I feel like I am in paradise.

My oldest brother is now a sergeant, the next oldest is an electrical engineer and I am nothing, but I am richer in experience than any of my brothers, and that has some value. Now I am home and have it good for a time and have honestly earned it. I have gone through the gauntlet. Granted, mostly while young, but at my older age, I am now at a standstill and that too, is going through hell fire and that becomes even worse.

Albrekt's Brother Konrad

Yesterday January 25, 1918

I have now been home for six weeks and it goes fairly well to be idle. I have accepted several invitations out to people's homes, but people don't have much to offer in these difficult times. It is market day here every Wednesday and when the farmers come to the market with their produce, people go out halfway to meet them and buy their produce. If you want to buy anything from them, you have to be at the market at dawn, otherwise everything is sold out. For my part, I don't need anything they have because I am idle most of the time and don't eat as much as for example a man that does heavy work.

I have been in Jonkoping a few days. I was in a shave and haircut salon to get my haircut. I will now make a comparison between a barbershop in Sweden and a barbershop in America. First the American shop with two barbers. As soon as you come inside the door, a barber greets you and invites you to sit down. When it is your turn you sit in the barber chair that is so constructed that by turning a handle the chair can be put in any position the barber wants, high or low, laying down, or sitting upright. After you sit down, you then say if you want to haircut or shave or both. The hair is cut first and then the chair is put in a laying position and the barber lathers and shaves you and then puts you in a sitting position and shaves the back of your neck. He washes off the soap, rubs an ointment on so your skin does not chap and at last puts on some powder you then pay and go.

Now we will take a shave and get a haircut in a salon in Sweden. When you come, you see the barber standing in long white coats. One cuts and the other shapes. You then say hello and get a graceful nod from one of those mighty matadors. When your turn comes you go to the one that shaves first and get lathered up by the apprentice, a little guy about 10 or 11 years old. He lathers your face with his hand and does not use a brush like they do in America. The chair is a regular chair with a backrest and armrests and a small rest at the back of the chair for your head. After you are lathered up, the arrogant journeyman comes in shaves you. He makes some mighty swings with the razor in a little while he is finished and says "vassego". That means you can get up and wash yourself in a basin of water the best that you can. I did not want to shave, so I went to the one that clips. He asked if he should use the clipper and then proceeded on my poor skull as if he was going to rub away my whole head. I thought several times that I should get up and go, but did not want to create a scene, so I sat still until the terrifying torture was over, but then I also look like a half-brother to an old man. My whole neck was shaved up over the ears and the top of my head had a little hair that was left and that was smeared with a cosmetic so that I look like a licked calf. I also want to add, that when I got home I washed my hair with genuine American shampoo to get out the sticky cosmetic. I cannot stand hair that is sticky.

I saw "VARMLANNINGARNA" (a play) in the theater. It was a fine play and well done. The nicest part about it was that they did not show a movie before the play like they do in America.

January 30, 1918

I will now write a little about conditions here in Malmback and start with the food. It is not so easy to get coffee or tea except in a café or Konditori. If for example you want to buy a cup of coffee, it costs $.50 for 2 cups and only one lump of sugar, cream you can get as much as you want, cake or biscuits can be had without a ration card and are mostly composed of air, a little sugar and egg white and no flour in them. You can easily eat 20 such baked goods and a couple cups of coffee and the sweets cost $.20 each.

There is now meat rationing. Each person is allowed to hundred 50 g a week to manage with, after that you do whatever you want. If you buy direct from the farmer, you can get a side of beef for $2.10 a kilo. If you buy so-called bone free, it cost $2.70 a kilo. Potatoes cost $10.50 a ton. Beef costs four crowns a kilogram. It has been as much as 20° below zero here in Malmback and now it has been mild for over a week. It is so mild that almost all the snow is melted and we had plenty of snow.

February 22, 1918

I almost forgot to write in my book but now it will be. People that use tobacco have a difficult time to get these items. A shipment came to Malmback on the 4 o'clock train. People stood in line outside the stores until most of it was gone. They had been out of tobacco for a week and it is already gone for most of the stores and no more will be sent until the middle of March. A little soap, if you can find some, cost one crown. Real soap is not to be found, but surrogate soap is two or three crowns a kilo. I bought some wash powder surrogate the other night and paid $1.25 for a small packet. I could've bought such a packet in the United States for $.10 no cost $.25 a liter and they cost just as much or 25 ore a kilo. We bought some hay the other day for our cow that I carried home in sacks. I was out and cut some heather for the cow. It is a meager diet for her but if it holds her until spring it will get much better.

I did some painting yesterday but did not like it. It strikes me as childish to stand there and poke with little round brushes. The method is different in the US. It does not surprise me at all that Swedes that have been in America do not stay home in Sweden. Everything here at home seems to me not worth the effort.

If I had 40 or 50,000 crowns, I would stay in Sweden, but now that I don't, I think it is best to go back to the USA. There it is possible for me to get a piece of land, but not here. A farm here cost 40 or 50,000 crowns. That is big enough to have a hired man and one that a husband-and-wife can manage cost about 25,000 crowns. Growing rice is the best type of farming. I have seen it and it could happen that I will try that sometime.

February 27, 1918

I was in Huderyd today and by grace was able to buy four sheaves of straw for one crown a sheaf. It is sad to think that here you have to feed straw and pay $.10 a kilogram if you're lucky enough to get it, and in America they burn it to get rid of it. There certainly was a crop failure this year and I think the soil is useless. It is only stone and moss. There are many that have paid $.50 per kilogram for hay here in Malmback and milk only cost 25 or for a liter. A liter and a kilogram are just about the same. If the war would end sometime, the farms would soon go down in price. Sound of hard cash will end for the farmers and wages will go slowly down so it will be a trade-off. It will be good times for the worker and poor times for the farmer. I think for my part, I will return to the USA as soon as I can, because no matter how you twist and turn the matter, America is better for the poor worker than in Sweden and the rich have it good no matter where they are.

March 29, 1918

I'm not going to make some observations of Sweden at this time. I did some painting in Sorang this week. I rode the train every morning and night and had some food with me. It was not like it used to be when you went out to the farm land. Before it was a real party, now there is not even a good cup of coffee unless you have sugar with you.

The paste that I use was something inferior that was cooked and put up in the barrel until ready for use. It scared you to look at it and it smelled of Lysol a long way off. It was full of lumps and most likely cooked from old wheat and other junk that could not be used for anything else but paste and other things. Instead of linseed oil, I had some oil that looked like dark syrup and was just as tenacious, and such tools they have here! They are considerably inferior to the American tool. For example, I use the brush that was 3 1/2 inches in diameter around the handle. It was a different story when I used the brush that I had with me from America. The other little brushes are okay for painting chairs, but for all the other painting they are worthless.

I have often wondered why the Swedish Americans do not stay here in Sweden, but it does not surprise me any longer because once they have become accustomed to American work tools and methods, it is childish and awkward here at home and to get them to understand that we have better methods in the US than here and to get them to use the same system here is very difficult.

To travel home and greet everyone for summer, I don't disapprove of, because it is homey here in Sweden and you can have it very nice if you have "Micke schaber" as the Jews said. Nature here is rich in animal and vegetation life and the climate nice and more. Think how nice I would have had it in the summer if (there comes that big IF) the times were normal and the person had plenty of money. It very well can happen that a person can have fun anyway. Yes, it has always been IF and BUT that has come into my life and will most likely be in the future also, as long as it does not take away one's sense of humor, things will go just as well.

April 21, 1918

It is a genuine fine Spring. The snow is almost gone and so is the ice. Judging by past Springs, it will be an extra fine growing season this year and is sorely needed as the food supply is low. The Germans must have been sinking the boats with a mighty force or else there is a news blackout in America now. It is now about five weeks since I have heard or seen anything in the newspapers from there. I have not had a single letter from the US since I came home.

It is hard to know how to talk to people here. It was not hard in the US. It was right to say "you" to everyone. Here it should be proper to say "you" to everyone, but to be proper here, a person should say "thou" to everyone, but that word is too fine to use out in the farm country because then you are regarded as being stuck up. When I first came home and met acquaintances they avoided talking to me direct and said, "they have come home now also, have you been a painter in America?" And so on. People that use these phrases would rather say "you" but don't know how it would be received. The most disturbing is when older people say "you" to me before and now say for example "Mister". Just about as dumb is the constant repeating of the name. No, in America it is much better. There you say "you" to everyone and it makes it easier to talk to anyone. Most Swedes regard "you" in the same sense as the Swedish word "ni". For my part, I think that "you" can serve for both "ni and du" in English, namely "thou" is used in the Bible and in prayer to God, but then practical life is never real.

September 15, 1918, Café in Malmback

It has been such a long time ago that I had my daybook out, that I hardly recognized her when I saw her. I have considered stopping to write anymore, but then I thought it would be nice to read when I get back to America and that I will most likely do sooner or later. I see that I have not written since 21 April and now we are in the middle of September.

I had made my mind up to tell the truth about everything when I got home, one time while I was in the barbershop, I met one of my former friends. He asked me if I hadn't scraped together at least $10,000 and I jokingly said that I had at least twice that amount, but he took me seriously and then I figured if that's what he wants to believe then let him. You do not lose by being considered a rich man. That spread like wildfire, that I had plenty of money. To confirm to the good people of Malmback in that belief, my fine fur coat made no insignificant contribution. I bought nice Christmas presents for my siblings and people thought they cost more than they did, consequently I am considered a wealthy man and as long as people hold that belief it goes good for me.

My sister Selma worked in a café and the woman that had it was married at Christmas and then in a meeting it was decided that Selma and Beda (the other girl) would take over the café. When it came to signing a lease, they had second thoughts, and decided to let it go. One time I just said to the building owner," you can just as well rent it out to me". That, he thought was a good idea. After thinking it over later, I decided it would not be so wrong after all. So I rented the café from him and came to an agreement with the girls that they would get half of the profit as wages and that I would get the other half would go to me for the capital that I was risking. The next thing to do was to settle up with Anna. I bought almost everything from her and got a good price. I then said to her that I wanted six months' credit on the furniture because I have my money in America and at the present time with the slow post system, it would take six months to get a bank draft here. That this money was not deposited in my name, she could not believe. I then thought that it is easy to do business if you are considered a wealthy man. Had she known what I knew, then I would not have gotten credit from her. Now I owe her 667 crowns and she does not have the slightest guarantee that she will get her money. Not a line is written concerning this, but 1 November, she will get her money even if I have to borrow it from my brother Konrad.

I believe I will earn 200 crowns a month and room and food since I started this business, and a better business I have never made. I am still not satisfied. I think it is so tedious here in Malmback. If only I was married, then I think I would thrive better. I could be married now, there are a couple of girls here, and if one of them was my wife, it would go well. There are many girls here that I think I could have, but only one that I want, and her, I don't think I could get. Even if I could get her, I don't know if I would, because I know that she would not travel to America. One that would be suitable for me must be one that would go with me anywhere into the hottest California if need be.

February 3, 1919

I have an impulse to write in my daybook a few lines, but hardly know what to write about. I see that I had girls on my mind the last time I wrote, and I also have a girl on my mind now. How I became acquainted with her I will explain below in English so that she cannot read it if she should come across this book. I saw her for the first time at the end of August and the Sunday between Christmas and New Year's we were engaged.

Agda Lundquist

Albrekt

There is starting to be a shortage of work in the chair factory here. They have not sold much in the way of chairs since Christmas, because the prices are too high. People are waiting for prices to come down before they buy. Before I left Sweden a rocking chair cost seven crowns, and the same chair now cost 56 crowns. That is an increase of 500%, so it is no wonder that people are waiting for the prices to come down. A somewhat good horse will cost 3000 crowns and it used to cost from 1 to 2000 crowns. Before the maximum price was set up, you could get 1500 crowns for a fat pig and from 7 to 14 crowns for a kilogram of bacon.

Surrogate flour was the only flour you could use in the café. It is ground rosehips and cost $4.50 a kilogram. I have bought this once in the spring, but when you can get real flour, like wheat, corn and oat flour from 1 to 3 crowns a kilo, then there is no idea to buy rosehips flour. If the authorities find out that you are using real flour, you can get into a jam for not doing your duty.

February 22, 1919

I have been in many communities both here and in America and such ill raised yokels that are here, I have never seen in any other place. It is the small boys that are the worst, but still it is that the older boys that encourage them and laugh at their immaturity. When the small boys see that they have the approval of the big boys, they become even more insolent. The most, at least of the big boys, do not approve of the smaller boy's rudeness, but do not dare to say anything, because no one wants to be the scapegoat and because the small tyrants rage. They do not like being called chicken.

They sit here in my café at night making noises. Up to now I have tried to handle them with mildness because I thought it would be better to give a boy a biscuit instead of a box in the ear. The biscuit he will soon forget, but he will never forget a box in the ear. Such a tactic may be possible to use with such people as these are, that have lost their sense of right and wrong. When you have boys such as these are, the only thing that helps is severity. Mildness I have tried and failed. Now I will try severity for a while. If I fail, the same system will apply anyway. I am forced to keep the café closed at night, otherwise it is too hard on my nerves, to be angry too often, and in the long run can have an effect on the nervous system. The problem is that when the café is closed to the animals, the decent people can't come in either.

NOTE: Albrekt did not write anymore until he returned to America in the month of June 1923

END OF BOOK 6

BOOK 7

RETURN TO AMERICA

June 29, 1923, Ridgeway, Canada

I left Malmback May 14 in the morning. Everything was more like a dream than reality, that I was separated from my wife and children and have no communication with them.

I stayed in Varnamo three hours and wrote home. I came to Goteborg at night and stayed at the hotel Britannia for two nights. I was out and looked at some of the exhibits in Goteborg, but got tired of walking around and for that part, I hardly remember what I saw, as my thoughts were of home. I left Goteborg on the steamship Balden 16 May and arrived in England the 18th. I stayed in Newcastle four hours and then left for Liverpool where I went on board the steamship Canada on 19 May. We landed in Québec Sunday the 27th and then to Montréal the same day, at night.

The journey went well, except in the North Sea, I got seasick. I was not at all seasick on the Atlantic. It was 12 o'clock when we came to Montréal. We then took a cab to the YMCA as it is called here. It was filled up, so they took us to the finest hotel in town, the Royal Hotel. It was nice, but much too nice for us. Two men slept in each room and paid $4.00 apiece. We were eight people altogether. An engineer from Norrland, a notary from Copenhagen, two young boys from Kiruna, two were from

Trollhatan and the one I was together with was from Goteborg, and then there was a fellow from Sundsvall who also had a wife and a full-grown son in Sweden.

We were about 20 Swedes on the boat, and almost all intended to go to the USA, but since there were so many of us, some could not go until after 1 July. Some had their passes signed in the States, and some didn't. I thought it would be possible to cross the border without any trouble. So, the line thinned out. I borrowed $10 from one of my comrades and bought a ticket to Buffalo, thinking we could cross over the border easily.

There were officers at the station that had gotten the news that we were going over, so they ordered us to the United States immigration office where we had to undergo the worst cross-examination that the worst criminal would not receive. I was the spokesperson for the other three boys that I was with. We were there the whole day and that night we learned that we could come back 1 June, and then they would file an application that we were to give to the consulate. Later, when they got a satisfactory answer from the consulate in Goteborg, we would be admitted but that would have cost $20 or $30 per man, and I was already almost out of money.

There was nothing else to do but to go to an employment agency and get work, and that we did. I got the promise of being a foreman on a railroad. If I could get 10 Swedish boys with me then I would be the foreman for them and get $100-$225 a month plus room and board. That sounded good, and then I thought that I would get some benefit from my ability to speak the language.

We got there 10 o'clock at night after a day's journey on the train and boat. The barrack was like a big box with a big iron stove in the middle, and around the sides were wooden boxes with the mattress and two blankets on each one. What these bedclothes were made of was hard to tell, because they were dirty and smelled awful. I was so tired that I could not go anywhere else, so there was nothing else to do but go to bed.

I thought that if the food was good then I could put up with the rest as long as the pay was good. In the morning, it turned out that the food was of the same quality as the lodging. Later when I told the boss that I was to be a foreman I got the answer that they have enough foreman now, so I had to work with the others for $.35 an hour and pay one dollar a day for the food.

We had a Norwegian foreman, but he was so good that you could not have better. He told us that we should take it easy so as not to get tired. The trip there cost $13, the German at the employment office got three dollars, and the food on the trip cost one dollar, so that was $13 to work off before you could have anything over, so the future was not so bright.

July 5, 1923

I will now continue about when I quit and left myself in the clay mire. During the time we worked, I proposed to Ejnar Andersson that he and I should (softly on our feet) at night, leave there. That he agreed to, but could not be quiet about our plan, and told the others and proposed that they should also leave.

My plan was, if Ejnar and I could get to a station and get to the border, then without trouble, we could get to Chicago. Now he wants more to go with us, but did not get more than one, a Northerner by the name of Trane to go with. We got our bags together at night, when the lights were off. We quietly snuck out of our bunks, first me, then the others. When we got outside, a worker came and asked me if we were going on our way. I said "yes". Ejnar had already run another way, so I had to find him but could not in the dark. When I came to the place where I left Trane and the Frenchman, he was gone. The Frenchman told him to stay but Trane did not understand him, all of a sudden, he bolted and ran off toward Villa Marie.

After the Frenchman waited a while and whistled and discussed the situation, there was nothing else to do but head out on the way, so I bid the Frenchman adieu and he wished me luck on my journey. When I had gone half a mile whistling, they answered and then I found them. They were standing and waiting for me and wondered if I was still in one piece. We set our course to Villa Marie and 1 o'clock at night, we came to a small town and then I was so tired that I could not go any further. A light was burning in a window and there is where we went. As luck would have it, two people were up holding a wake. The boss of that place had died. That we learned when we asked if we could buy milk and drink, but we couldn't because they would have to go through the room where the boss laid, to get to the cellar and they dared not. We stayed the night and slept good. That day we had a person in the hotel (if that was the new boss or who, I don't know, but he spoke English, the other man spoke only French) to drive us in a car to New Lisheard, and for that he got $18. That was expensive for a four-hour trip on a Saturday night. On Monday, I got work with the painter and Ejnar got work loading and unloading coal with a carrier.

That night he could not find out what time he should start in the morning, so I went with him and asked Brewer. He said 7 o'clock. I went to Davis's home and knocked but no one answered. After I had knocked a while, I went in anyway, since the door was not locked. I figured that they did not hear the knocking, but then an Englishman came and chased me out and was abusive, but I just said to him that he could pay me for the half day I had worked and then I would go. Go out he said, and come back at 8 o'clock.

I went back to the hotel and woke up Trane and told him that I quit. Later we went to Davis's and got my money. At night we decided, Trane, Ejnar, myself and another boy by the name of Augustson, that we would go out to the railroad, but for my part, I wanted to see if I could get a job painting from another painter in Cobalt. If I did not get work, I would go with them. Wednesday morning when we went to the restaurant the painter Davis was standing on the steps outside. I said hello to him, and he said hello back. I said to the other boys that if I just said half a word to Davis I could start work again, but that I did not do, but then Davis came in and wanted to talk to me and wondered if I would stay and work. Then I would get $.65 an hour. I then went home and put on my overalls and started again. That night when I got back to the hotel the boys had left. It was strange to be alone there, no Swede to talk to and no Swedish to read, but I had work for 10 hours a day and earned good money, and the third week went very well. I had figured that I had $56 coming on Saturday night. I then thought that I would quit and go to Windsor and try to get over to Detroit and so on back to Chicago, but these plans never happened. Thursday night Ejnar came back and talked about his hardships. When they left Cobalt and came to Cochrane, he sent his money home to Sweden. They took work on railroads in Cochrane and started working. After a few days, they did not dare stay any longer, because there were forest fires all around. They left their tents, utensils and the whole railroad hand car and went 30 miles to another railroad and got work. Ejnar wanted Augustson to go with him to a doctor because he was not feeling well, but that he did not want to do, so Ejnar went to Cobalt in hope of finding me. Augustson and Trane went in a different direction. Now there was nothing else to do but do as Augustson did. Let Ejnar shift for himself or get him a job. I paid him the six dollars he put out for me for the automobile ride and then we had to go to Toronto and both took a job with free travel, to shovel coal.

I thought that I had to stay at least a day to get him started, and then go my own way. We arrived at the regulation district at 10 o'clock and were shown into a luggage van to sleep. That was the promised housing. We crawled down in the dirty rags and went to sleep. During the night, there was a thunderstorm and the luggage van was not tight, so it rained on us.

It rained on Ejnar first. He laid in a bunk over me and said that he was getting rained on. I told him to move to another bunk. He moved to a bunk on the other side, but that mattress was torn. The wood shavings that the mattress was stuffed with fell down into the face of an Irish man that slept under him, and he started to swear. We then took our mattresses and laid on the floor and held our raincoats over our heads so that it would not rain on our faces.

We had to get up at 5:30 AM because we were laying in front of the Irishman's food cabinet. The food you had to prepare the best you could. The Irishman cooked coffee in a tin can and cooked eggs in the same can and ate like a pig. The table was full of egg shells, old canned food and ripped up pieces of bread. The floor had not been swept in living memory. After we had washed up we went to a restaurant and ate breakfast, and then back to the luggage van. The foreman came and wrote down our names. The employment agency had spelled my name Albrekt Sunurik so I spelled it correctly for the foreman so that he got it right. Later I swept off the table and the luggage van, so that it would be more tolerable. I then went to a store and bought coffee, sugar, cream, eggs, bread, coffee cups and spoons, and then cooked coffee in a coffee pot that I also bought. That was the best coffee we had since we left Sweden.

July 6

After we drank coffee, we went out on the town or more like a village. We went down to the Niagara River and on the other side we saw the town of Buffalo in the state of New York. I thought that we were like Moses when he saw the town that he could not come in.

We went back to the van again and there I suggested to Ejnar that we should go to the nearest town and I would find him a place with a farmer, and myself to go elsewhere. We took our picks and packs and quietly left and came to Ridgeway and got work in a stone crushing mill for $.45 an hour. I have now quit and plan on trying to get to Buffalo by boat, and if I get there, I will head for Chicago as fast as possible to see **Jack Malmquist 5340 Montrose Ave., Chicago, IL**

I got myself ready in the morning for the trip to Buffalo and went down to Crystal Beach and bought a return ticket to Buffalo. That I got without any trouble. When the boat came in and they started to board I went with but then the passageway got narrower and narrower until only one at a time could pass. All of a sudden, a man hollered to me and wanted to talk to me. He asked me all sorts of questions and wrote down a card as fast as I answered. He told me that if I wanted to go to USA I had to have my visa stamped and pay an immigration tax of $18. I then was advised that there was no idea in paying if I didn't want to stay in the USA but if I did want to stay, then the idea was that I would not have to fear being refused.

Just think, if I would've had the money to go direct from Sweden to Chicago! Now there was nothing else to do but turn around. I am now thinking of going to Windsor. I want to at least get as close to Chicago as possible. If I can find work in my trade then I can just as well be in Windsor as Chicago but I don't know if there are any Swedes in Windsor who will accept me and if I am right for work there, most likely the wages are lower than in Chicago.

My old bad luck forces me to be gracious, but I don't want to complain as long as I can stay healthy. Just so my wife and children are healthy and I can see them again, but that too, is taking longer than I had thought. Had Ejnar not come, I would have been in Windsor two weeks ago. If I leave at 6 o'clock I should be there by 11 o'clock at night and then in the morning, I can see if I can find work.

July 14 Chicago

I left Ridgeway as I planned at 5 o'clock in the morning the ticket cost $7.70. I changed trains in Brantford. In London, a couple of boys got on that I understood were Scandinavians but I was not sure, so I waited a while before I talked to them. They did not know that I was Scandinavian, because they went to a young boy and asked him how far it was to Chicago, but he did not understand them. I then interrupted and asked if they were Swedish, but they were Norwegians. They were on the way to Chicago the same as me, so they had tickets only as far as Windsor.

When we got to Windsor at 12 o'clock at night we rented a hotel room. The day after we went out to see if there was any possibility of getting over to the other side. For my part I saw that it would be hard if not impossible. The next night, the two Norwegians decided that they would "loan" a boat and row over to the other side. They wanted me to go with, but my principles against such an invitation held me back. I thought it would be better if I stayed and looked for work in Windsor. We left the hotel at 1 o'clock at night. Each Norwegian had a package in a big knapsack with him. I went with them anyway until we came to a restaurant where we went in and had coffee. We later parted company and how it turned out for them I don't know.

In the morning, I felt alone and almost sorry that I had stayed behind. I thought that I would try to find someone to smuggle me over. So, I walked nice and calm along the bank of the river. After I had walked a short way I saw two boys sitting on a bench casting longing glances toward Detroit. I sat down on the next bench and tried to hear some of their conversation, but they talked so low that it was impossible. After a while I walked over and asked what the time was, one of them took out his watch and let me see for myself. I spoke Swedish and learned that they were Norwegian and had been in Canada two months on their way to the USA and up into now had no luck in getting there.

I suggested to them that we should go further North up the river and try to get over, because there were too many houses between Windsor Detroit on both sides. We went to a bookstore and there they had a big map in the window. On the map, I saw that the river was about the same width 80 miles north as where we were, about 200 feet. We all agreed to travel there.

We were now four in the party. The Norwegians had another friend. We took the train to Chothong, and then a streetcar to Wallaceberg and stayed there and ate supper. Later we took a cab to Port Lambton. That was right on the river, and we then spent the night in the Hotel Victoria.

July 24

In the morning, I went far out along the side of the river to see if there was any way to cross over, but it did not look very promising. When I got back to the hotel, the owner had asked the Norwegian boys if they wanted to cross the river. When they said yes, he told them that there was a man in Port Lambton that used to smuggle people across, but they could not learn anymore because they were not that good with the language. As soon as I had a chance, I talked to the hotel owner and he directed me to a fisherman by the name of Hinton. I went to him right away. At first, he was very uncooperative, but when he got a promise of being well-paid he told me to go home and he would follow after. After I was back at the hotel for a while he came and asked how much we could pay. I told him that we could pay $5.00 apiece. He thought that was good and that we should go right away. He said that it was easier to cross during the day than at night, because during the day they don't keep as close a watch.

We all took our knapsacks and walked down the railroad tracks and met Hinton in front of his house. We paid him his high price and then laid down in the bottom of the boat, so as not to be seen, in case some "guys" were out looking around. Two Indians rowed us across with powerful pulls on the oars to the other side. People sat in their windows watching and laughing.

When we came over the river, we went into a group of oak trees and rested a while.

We then took a streetcar direct to Detroit. That cost $.88. I then took the first train from Detroit to Chicago and got there in the morning. I took a cab to Jakob but that was dumb because that cost $3.25 and all I had was Canadian money and the driver would not take that, so I had to borrow the money from Jakob's landlord.

August 21

I have now worked five weeks in Chicago painting and bronzing radiators. It is work that must go fast, but it is not so fussy. I don't like it much but I think I can find something better here in Chicago. The pay is so high that I have never earned so much before namely $1.25 an hour. That is different than what they pay in Malmback, namely 72 ore.

I had to join the trade union to get work, and that cost me $100. I took a different job then I started on Monday but that was worse than painting radiators. I was washing ceilings and walls. That was for Nylund and Thurander, but it was not something I wanted to continue with. So today I went and painted radiators again. I don't know if the bosses know whether I worked Monday or not because I have not seen them today but in the morning, I will probably see them and hear what they have to say. I have just written a letter to Nylund and Thurander that I want to be paid for the day I worked for them.

February 12th, 1924 Chicago Illinois

I have been here seven months now and have earned $1500. Those are the best earnings I have ever had. I was thinking tonight that if I ever get so far as to get our house in Malmback paid it should be called "Segerlon" (tough victory) because if it gets paid my wife and I have had a tough time of it, and have earned our house in a tough victory. It has been a struggle to build it, but maybe I will think of a more fitting name if we ever come so far as to move in and not have a bank loan that hangs like Damocle's sword over us all the time. I got my money from Nylund and Thurander in a letter. The Johnsons don't know that I was gone for a day, so everything is going its merry way, just like before.

February 17, 1924 Chicago Illinois

When a person has a kind of job I have, you have plenty of time to think. Most the time I am alone and have no one to talk to. Most of the time I think about the future and that, I painted in bright colors and that is better than painting in dark colors. The future prospects I set up are not so high that they cannot become a reality.

Since I came to Chicago I have had steady work and earn $10 a day so in seven months I've been here I have earned $1701.25. That is not bad for seven months. In Swedish money that is 6379 Crowns at the rate of exchange of 3.75 Crowns to a dollar. If I had that money it would not be bad but I only have about $100. The rest is going to support me and my family, rent payments to the bank, rent for me and paying off debts and more. Sometimes I figure that if I stay with the Johnsons for six years and earn $2860 a year I should be able to save $1800 a year. If I put that in the bank and draw 3% interests, by the spring of 1930 that would be $11,642. In Swedish money that is 43,657.50 Crowns.

So much should be possible in six years through steady work and saving, providing one has their health and are able to work. If this money is used wisely it should be possible to live in Sweden and be independent.

Maybe that would be dismal to work and save that long and have such work that you have no control over yourself, but to be like a machine or something similar. I think I would rather stay here until 1 October. By that time, we could have $1150 saved and then go to California and lease a rice farm and maybe have 43,000 crowns in six years and be your own boss and operate and decide as you want, and not have to sit in a corner five days a week chewing on a sandwich for lunch, but able to go by my wife and eat well prepared food at a table. If my plans become a reality which I hope they do, then we will settle up our debts, finish the house and rent it out for the highest possible rent. I'm coming to the end of the train of thought, that would be most satisfying. My highest interest is not dancing, drinking, playing cards, hunting, fishing or playing golf, but to build a house for ourselves to live in. I want to build on a paid-up lot in Malmback where it is beautiful for example, between the woods and Malmstens. That house I will build in the old farm style and it will have a laundry room, food cellar, veranda and an entrance hall (at least 10 x 14'), work room, kitchen, bath and four bedrooms.

I will do most of the work myself using my own methods. The inner wall will be plastered on light reed mats and the outer walls will be cobblestone and brick mortar. The frame will be raised up using the American method, with two by fours with 5 inch nails driven into the two by fours 2 inches and into the mortar 3 inches. That will be a strong house in a house that does not have to be painted or replastered. The stone I can get for nothing, because there's plenty of stone in Smaland.

The dining room will have checkered parquet floor of oak and the veranda will have a cement floor with black and white or black and red squares. The dining room will have a kakelugn big enough to heat there. One of the largest that can be found, with a big fireplace that begins no higher than 6 inches above the floor. In front of the kakelugn will be cement tiles the same size as the oak tiles in the floor.

There is much more I could figure in, but that will do for now. However, that is my highest ambition- - to build such a house and I know my wife's highest ambition would be to decorate it inside with hard work that she has done herself. If truth is found in work and lasting contentment, then I should have it, then I can I work when I want to, and quit working when I want.

END OF BOOK 7

EPILOGUE

Written by Arne Lundquist **2003**

Chicago Illinois 1923 to 1995

Albrekt returned to the US in 1923 and landed in Chicago intending to continue to California. He found work in his own trade and earning good money decided to stay in Chicago. Agda, Jergen and Clarence left their home in Malmback and joined him in the year 1924. He bought a lot and built a small house in the year 1926 at 7719 W. Farragut in Chicago. Arthur the first American-born, was born on Montrose Avenue in 1925 in a rented house. Arne was born in the new house in 1927. Charles was born in the hospital in 1929. Sven was born at home on Farragut Avenue in 1931. Roy was also born at home in 1933, Francis the only girl and the last child, was also born at home on Farragut Avenue in 1935. His family was now complete and work was plentiful up to the "crash" of 1929. Albrecht had quite a bit of money in the bank and in stock, which he then lost. The whole country went into a deep depression and many people became unemployed.

The depression years were hard times in the USA. In order to provide for such a large family, Albrekt bought a cow and raised chickens, thus we had milk, eggs, cheese and meat. The vegetable garden in the summer provided vegetables for canning as well as fruit. Albrekt continued in his trade and at times worked for the government painting schools, post office buildings and the like.

The U.S.A. became involved in World War II on December 7, 1941, with Japan and later with Germany and Italy a few months later. Jergen was called into service and served four years in the Army Air Force in India. Clarence and Arthur served in the Army in Europe and took part in many battles with the German forces. They also took part in the freeing of prisoners in the German death camps. Arne served in the U.S. Navy and spent his time in the Pacific and nine months on the island of Guam. The war ended August 8, 1945. All four boys returned home, and none were injured. All four boys married and started their own families in the next few years. Charlie was the next to serve in the Korean conflict in the Army from 1950 to 1952. Sven was exempt from service due to stomach ulcers. Roy, the last to serve, spent four years in the Army Air Force mostly in Tripoli from 1952 to 1966

By the year 1960 all siblings were married and raising their own families. Albrekt died on the 31st of October, 1963 of a heart attack at home, in his own bed, at the age of 74. Agda died 10 years later at the age of 79. Both are resting at Memory Gardens in Arlington Heights Illinois. Jergen died in 1981 and is resting in Elmhurst Illinois. Sven died in 1985. Arthur died in 1992 and Clarence died the same year. Clarence, Arthur and Sven are all resting in Memory Gardens in Arlington Heights Illinois.

There are a total of 25 grandchildren and 33 great grandchildren at the present time (2003). Albrekt had been retired for 10 years at the time of his death.

(Post script: Arne died April 14, 2009, and Charlie died exactly one week to the day after him. Both are also resting in Memory Gardens)

Albrekt Lundquist Family

Left to right rear row: Clarence, Jorgen, Arthur, Arne, Charles

Middle: Roy, Agda, Albrekt, Sven

Front: Frances

ALBREKT FAMILY PHOTOS I

Albrekt and Agda

Agda

ALBREKT FAMILY PHOTOS II

Albrekt's Father and Mother, Ola Persson and Amanda Nilsdotter

Albrekt, parents, brothers and sisters

CPSIA information can be obtained
at www.ICGtesting.com
Printed in the USA
LVHW03s2141180618
581184LV00001B/39/P